C000221506

Rocket Girls

Sam Gold and the Case of the Missing Uranium

The Case of the Missing Uranium

* * *

Melanie Fine

ROCKET GIRLS PRESS / LOS ANGELES

Copyright © 2021 by Melanie Fine.

All rights reserved. No part of this publication may be reproduced, distributed or transmitted in any form or by any means, including photocopying, recording, or other electronic or mechanical methods, without the prior written per-mission of the publisher, except in the case of brief quotations embodied in critical reviews and certain other noncommercial uses permitted by copyright law. For permission requests, write to the publisher, addressed "Attention: Permissions Coordinator," at the address below.

Melanie Fine/Rocket Girls Press
1480 S. Wooster St. Suite 1
Los Angeles, CA 90035

www.RocketGirls.com

Cover Art by Caitie Ford @caia.moon http://www.caiamoon.co.uk/

Publisher's Note: This is a work of fiction. Names, characters, places, and incidents are a product of the author's imagination. Locales and public names are sometimes used for atmospheric purposes. Any resemblance to actual people, living or dead, or to businesses, companies, events, institutions, or locales is completely coincidental.

Ordering Information: Special discounts are available on quantity purchases by corporations, associations, and others. For details, contact the publisher at the address above.

Los Angeles / Melanie Fine Author — First Edition

ISBN 9798518673632

Printed in the United States of America

Sign up to be a
Rocket Girl at
https://rocketgirls.com

Receive news of new releases, science
activities, and stories in your inbox.

Contents

Sam Gold and the Case of the Missing Uranium

The Science Behind It

Science Experiments and Activities

Glossary

For all the curious girls who love to play with rockets, microscopes, and chemistry sets.

And most of all, for my own Rocket Boy, Max.

1

The First Day of School

"**S**am! Einstein peed in the house again!"

Hearing the sound of my brother's voice was enough to rile me up for the day.

"I'm brushing my teeth!" I yelled back, though I had done that five minutes before. The truth was, I was staring at myself in the mirror, trying to brush back an unfortunate curl that insisted on drooping down the middle of my forehead. It was the first day of eighth grade and the last thing I wanted to do was look like a dork.

"Sam! You have to do something about your contraption!" another voice yelled from downstairs. It was my dad. "How many times have I told you to just walk the dog! It would do both of you a lot of good."

I cringed. I don't like being yelled at. Especially since the "contraption" my dad's referring to is a Raspberry Pi 4 Model B with a 1.5-GHz quad-core processor and 8GB of RAM. That's geek-speak for totally awesome computing power. I attached a motion sensor to the doggie door which is supposed to read the RFID chip on Einstein's collar and cause the door to open. And it works — most of the time, that is.

This curl was not doing what I needed it to do, so I added a handful of my brother's gel and combed it back. That oughtta do it... except that I now smelled like the department store's men's cologne aisle.

"I'll be right down!" I said. I grabbed my new backpack filled with fresh notebooks, pencils, and paper and bounded down the stairs.

There was the puddle, waiting for me. "You couldn't clean this up yourself?" I asked Alex who was smugly looking at me from behind his stack of pancakes.

"Why should I clean it up?" he replied. "It's your mess."

"Don't drag your brother into this," my dad added.

It's times like these that I greatly disliked my little brother. And the thought of him starting Taft Middle School this year meant my safety zone was being breached, big time. Yeah, it was only going to be for one year, as I'll be starting high school next fall, but it was already promising to be a very long year indeed.

I passed him as I got some paper towels and floor cleaner from the kitchen. "You're not walking with me to school you know," I said to him.

"Like I'd ever," he replied.

Humph. I cleaned the floor quickly and heard the menacing click of Alex's camera. "Don't you dare," I said to Alex who was now standing inches away from me, taking one shot, then too, and then a whole flurry of them.

"Oh, I dare," he said. "These are going in the yearbook."

"Dad!" I called out.

"You two, cut it out," my father said, as he brought my pancakes to the table. It was a long standing Gold family tradition to have pancakes on the first day of school. It was one of my favorite things about today, but it would have to wait.

I called Einstein over to me. Yes, he was still wearing his chip. I nudged him to the doggie door, and nothing happened. The door didn't move. I disconnected the Raspberry Pi from its cradle and threw out the dirty towels on my way upstairs to check on the problem.

"Where are you going now? Hurry up or you'll be late for your first day of Mrs. Cooper's class," my dad called after me.

I didn't bother telling my dad that I didn't have Mrs. Cooper until after lunch, but he was right about one thing. Mrs. Cooper's 8th Grade Science class was the thing of legends. Science was my favorite subject, and she had a way of teaching that got even the most reluctant kids to love science. Rumor had it that she had even taught one Nobel Prize winner and two astronauts. I fancied that maybe I'd be next.

I plugged the Raspberry Pi's USB into my computer and opened its coding software. I re-compiled the code to see if it would give me any errors. No errors. I then brought the RFID chip to its sensor on the Raspberry Pi. Its green LED light signaled that it recognized the chip. So why wasn't it working? Maybe the doggie door itself was the problem.

"Sam!" my Dad called from downstairs. "You're going to be late for school!" Looking at the time, I knew he was right. And yet I never liked to leave the scene of a problem without having figured out its solution. But it was 7:48 am. School started at 8 am and I lived a 9-minute walk away. There was barely enough time to get to school, let alone use my locker. And besides, Andrea was probably waiting for me at the corner.

I ran back downstairs. My brother Alex appeared to have already left. I grabbed my backpack and a pancake from the table, said "Bye Dad," and walked out the door.

Andrea wasn't at the corner. She probably got tired of waiting for me. I'd explain when I got to school. I quickened my pace to make sure I got to her before school started... which was gonna be any minute.

2

Locker Buddies

When I reached my locker, Andrea was there waiting for me.

Andrea's family had moved to Willowbrook from El Salvador last year. She'd tell me stories of what life was like there. I couldn't believe how different things were in another country, having never stepped foot out of this one. In a way, she was my saving grace. I had always felt like an outsider here, like I didn't belong. Andrea, being new to the school and new to the country, felt the same. It was as if we bonded over necessity. But the thing was, we really dug each other. Even when her English was poor and my Spanish even poorer, we just kinda got along. And have pretty much been inseparable ever since.

"Where were you?" Andrea asked, in a playful accusatory tone.

"I was trying to fix Einstein's RFID chip again," I explained.

I envied her long straight black hair, as I tried to smooth back the wayward curl that had popped free out of its holding gel.

"Why don't you just give up on that thing already?" she asked.

"Why don't you just give up on singing?" I asked.

She smiled. Point taken. Andrea had the most exquisite voice I'd ever heard, like an angel's. I could listen to her sing along with the Top 40 all afternoon long. She wanted to become a professional singer and I always kidded with her that I'd be able to say 'I knew her when...'

"Speaking of which, I finally figured out the song I'm going to audition with this afternoon."

Her audition for the most prestigious singing group at Taft, the Madrigal Singers, was today after school.

"Are you geeks gonna move or what?" said a familiar voice.

Both Andrea and I looked up at Kimberly Newhouse, the most popular girl in school, along with David Henry, the quarterback of the football team and her boyfriend, and Trish Cunningham, her bestie and captain of the Lacrosse team.

"Oh, sorry Kimberly," I said, quickly making room for her. Evidently Kimberly's locker assignment was right next to mine.

"I see we're locker neighbors," I said, trying to make small talk. As soon as the words flew out of my mouth, however, I knew they shouldn't have. Andrea knocked me on the shoulder confirming the mistake I'd made. It was an unwritten rule - you don't make small talk with the most popular girl in school.

"Look at the geek stating the obvious!" she said loudly to her two companions, and anyone else who could hear her — which was everyone in the hallway and probably two hallways past this one.

I sheepishly looked at Andrea.

"What's with the curl down her forehead?" she laughed to her friends. "She looks like a nursery rhyme. 'There was a little girl who had a little curl.'"

Her companions cracked up as did everyone else within earshot. I was so embarrassed I could have hidden inside my locker if there were room. I tried again to smooth the curl into submission.

As the three of them walked away, my embarrassment turned to anger. Why did I get so tongue-tied in front of them? Why didn't I stand up for myself?

"I'm gonna get even with her if it's the last thing I do," I said to Andrea.

"Forget about them. They're not worth it," Andrea said. "Besides, I didn't tell you what song I was going to sing."

"I wonder how I could rig up my Raspberry Pi to shock her every time she went for her locker," I said, my mind racing with retribution scenarios.

"Yeah, but then I'd only get to see you on visiting day at the Willowbrook Home for Wayward Girls."

That made me laugh. "Only if I get caught."

"Besides, I didn't tell you what song I'm auditioning with," Andrea said. "'Beautiful' by Christina Aguilera."

I stopped plotting for a moment and took it in. "'Beautiful' was our song. We'd sing along with it like no one was listening. And Andrea never gave me a hard time about my voice, unlike Mrs. Wyatt, the choir teacher, who told me on more than one occasion, "It'd be better if you just mouthed the words, Samantha."

"What is that smell?" Andrea asked, jerking me back from memory lane.

"What smell?" I asked.

"Is it you? You smell like a football player!" Andrea exclaimed, sniffing in my direction.

"Wow, nice thing to say to your best friend," I told her.

"No, not like that."

Again, I attempted to smooth back my curl, even more self-conscious. The warning bell rang before I got a chance to answer.

"We gotta go," I said, dialing my locker's combination. I put most of my books inside except for English and history, which I had next. "First person to the cafeteria saves a seat."

"See you later," Andrea said as she rushed off to class.

I tried to pull the curl down toward my nose to get a whiff of how bad the gel smelled. The curl wasn't quite long enough. And I didn't have time to stop by the bathroom to wash it out as the tardy bell rang. Late for my first class! I slammed my locker and ran to class, still plotting my revenge.

3

Revenge is a Dish Best Served Cold

B y the time I made it to the front of the cafeteria line, nearly 10 minutes of lunch period had passed. Usually, I pack myself a lunch in the morning, but I had other things on my mind. Besides, I sort of liked the two scoops of spaghetti and green beans. I tried to pass on the milk but Greta the lunch lady always made sure I took it. How she didn't notice the wasted cartons of milk littering the tables after lunch is beyond me.

Andrea was looking more annoyed than usual by the time I'd reached our table.

"Want my milk?" I asked her, knowing the answer, yet trying to distract from my tardiness. I took my milk off my tray and put it in the center of the table for anyone to take.

Deon and Freddy were finishing up by the time I sat down. "Hey Deon, Freddy," I said, acknowledging their presence.

"Hey Sam," replied Deon.

"Hey," replied Freddy.

"What do you two think of this -- sending Kimberly Newhouse a singing telegram from Ronald Willis smack in the middle of second period?"

Ronald Willis was the kid who always sat by himself. And, though we were all a little weird, he was just... well... weirder. He lived alone with his grandma. No one knew what had happened to his parents, but the rumors around Taft pretty much cast Ronald as a serial killer. There was no way they were true. At least... I didn't think so.

"What for?" Deon replied.

"Why not?" I responded incredulously.

"You'd get in a whole mess of trouble," Freddy said.

"She'd never know it was me. Besides," I added without skipping a beat, "I was hoping you two would do it for me."

"Do what?" Deon asked. "Order the singing telegram? Us?"

"No, sillies," Sam continued. "Do the singing telegram."

"You've got the wrong suckers," said Freddy.

"But you two sing so beautifully. And don't you want to get even with Kimberly?"

I didn't need to go into the reasons for getting even with Kimberly. They were manifold. Like the time last year when she started the rumor that Freddy's hair was actually a wig. People were tugging at his hair for months after.

"Not in a way that would make fools out of us," Deon said.

"Well, if you two won't do it, who will?" I asked, thinking aloud.

"Sam, I've been waiting all this time to talk to you and you're still thinking of Kimberly Newhouse," Andrea said.

"OK, talk to me." I said to her as I dug my spork into the first scoop-shaped mound of spaghetti.

"How you can eat that stuff is beyond me," she replied, trying to get back at me.

"Hey, I don't go to your house and insult your food."

"Yeah, sorry. Anyway, I was hoping we could peel away at the end of lunch so I could try my audition piece on you. But now there's barely any time left before the bell."

"I've heard you sing the song a thousand times."

"I know, but I've done some things with it that I wanted you to hear."

I checked my watch. "Is there time after school?"

"Probably not before the audition. And I'll probably be way too nervous."

"I'm sorry," I said. "How can I make it up to you? We're still going to the IMAX after school tomorrow, right?"

My mom worked as a research scientist at the Museum of Natural History which had its own IMAX, and I could go whenever I wanted. Besides, there was a new Hubble

Space Telescope movie I wanted to see that looked into the origins of the Universe.

"I wouldn't miss it!" said Andrea.

The school bell rang loudly, probably because the speaker was mounted directly over the table.

"See ya Sam," Freddy said as he and Deon took their trays to the counter.

"All I'm saying is to think about it, okay?" I yelled after them, above the noise of hundreds of students getting up for period 5.

I didn't get a response. Maybe it wasn't my best plan. But there were plenty where they came from.

"What's your next class?" I asked Andrea as we got up to go.

"PE," she said with a grimace. "How about you?"

"Mrs. Cooper!" I said, excited about finally getting to take the class that everyone refers to as the best.science.class.ever. No wonder Mrs. Cooper was being named Teacher of the Year. But the fact that it was now official made it even better. Andrea waited for me to put my tray away and we left the cafeteria together.

"Do you know that every student who's gotten to be her lab tech has gone on to do great things in science? Like the astronaut Rebecca Carlson, and Peter Smith who developed the Ebola vaccine. I'm going to be next!" I said. I was so excited about my next class that I left my backpack in the cafeteria. I waved Andrea to class and ran back to the cafeteria to pick up my stuff.

PARENTS JUST DON'T GET IT

By the time I got there, the doors were locked.

"Darn!" I shook on the doors to see if I could get the attention of the cafeteria workers inside. No one responded. I pounded on the doors. Still no answer. I was going to be late to my first day in Mrs. Cooper's class and yet I couldn't show up without my stuff.

The custodian's office wasn't far from the cafeteria, so I rushed over there to see if Earl was around. Earl had been working at Taft since it first opened. His two sons had long since graduated. His firstborn was in the military. And his second son went to Stanford Law and had become a big time attorney in D.C. He loved to share stories about the famous Washington politicians his son would meet.

There was no one in his office by the time I arrived. The tardy bell rang. It was official. I was now late to fifth period. What was I going to do?

I left the office dejected, resigned to show up not only late to Mrs. Cooper's, but without my materials. Not a great first impression. As I walked out to the quad toward the science building, I was elated to see Earl coming in my direction.

"Sam, you know better than to be late to class. Now hurry on! Never put your education on the back burner!"

"Earl, I'm so glad to find you!" I said. "I left my backpack in the cafeteria and now it's locked."

"I'm going in that direction Sam. Why don't you hurry to class and I'll bring it to you?"

I gave him the "no deal" look. He hesitated. And then said, "OK, let's hurry. But remember, never put your education on the back burner, backpack or not."

This was Earl's classic phrase. I'd heard it for two years, and now I heard it twice on the first day of my third year. I got the message.

We rushed to the cafeteria. Earl pulled what seemed like hundreds of keys from a cable attached to his belt, selected one, and unlocked the door. I rushed in, was grateful that my backpack was just where I left it, slung one strap over my shoulder and ran out.

"Thanks Earl, I owe you one!" I said to him as I ran ahead to the science building.

If Earl would ever call on the number of IOUs the students of Taft had leveled upon him, he'd be a very rich man indeed.

4

Not an Auspicious Start

I quietly opened the door to Mrs. Cooper's science lab, hoping to slink in unnoticed. It wasn't one of my most well thought-through plans. Mrs. Cooper had already begun her lesson which meant that she probably had already taken roll.

She looked up at me as I entered. I could feel the blood drain from my face.

"You must be Ms. Gold," she said to me.

"Y-y-yes," I said. "Sorry I'm late." I could feel all eyes on me.

"Take a seat. Class begins at 12:35. Not a minute later." And she went back to her lesson.

There were no seats available. That wasn't entirely true. There was one seat. But it was filled with stuff. Kimberly Newhouse's stuff. I would just as well stand in the back.

Mrs. Cooper looked at me again. My effort to be unobtrusive was failing, miserably. "Ms. Gold, do I need to ask you again to take your seat?"

"No, Mrs. Cooper," I said. And I walked over to the seat currently occupied by Kimberly Newhouse's stuff. I had been looking forward to this day for two years and now I was forced to sit next to Kimberly Newhouse, my sworn enemy. It seemed as if Kimberly felt the same way. She did not seem in a hurry to move her stuff. She slowly moved her backpack and set it atop the lab table. She then reluctantly picked up her purse and put it next to her backpack. Though I now had room to sit, her things took up much of my desk space, so much so that I had to peer through her backpack strap to see Mrs. Cooper. I adjusted my stool to make a little more distance between me and Kimberly's stuff -- and Kimberly.

"As I was saying," picking up from she had left off, "for each unit, you will be assigned a project to complete and a partner to complete it with." She could sense the inaudible moans coming from her students. This was not her first rodeo. "I know that you'd rather pick your own partners, and some of you would rather work on your own. The thing is, that's not the way the world works in general, and not the way science works in particular. Science is a collaborative effort. You must learn to work well with others."

Please, don't team me up with Kimberly.

Please, don't team me up with Kimberly.

I repeated in my head, over and over again.

"Your partner for the first unit is sitting right next to you. We'll change seats with each new project."

Just my luck, I thought to myself.

"Kimberly," Mrs. Cooper said, "would you help me distribute these boxes to each lab table?"

Kimberly got up and handed a black box to each table.

"How do we as scientists know what we know?" Mrs. Cooper asked. "After all, the atom, the basic building block of matter, was invisible to the eye when it was discovered. So, scientists had to use other tools at their disposal to observe and make predictions. Today, like good scientists, we're going to make observations too," Mrs. Cooper said. Kimberly returned to her seat with a smug air of superiority. "One person from each table will be the recorder, writing down your team's observations. Your task is to identify what's in each of your boxes without looking inside. Once you think you know the answer, sketch a picture of it on the same paper."

"Take out a piece of paper and be the recorder," Kimberly told me. I hated being told what to do. Yet I opened my binder and took out a piece of paper all the same.

She started shaking the box. "It makes 'thunk' noises as it hits the side of the box." Noticing that I wasn't writing down her every word, she exclaimed, "Write that down!"

Oh brother. I begrudgingly wrote it down.

"It seems to roll... and then slide - a combination of rolling and sliding."

I wrote her words down.

"Let me try," I said, reaching for the box.

"I'm not finished with it yet," she said, pulling the box away from me.

"Ok class, finish making your observations, and at the count of three, I'm going to have you pass the boxes clockwise," Mrs. Cooper demonstrated clockwise with her hand, "to the next table."

"One, two, three." Kimberly passed the box on to the next table. I never even got a chance to hold it. Luckily, the table to my left passed their box to me, and I certainly wasn't going to hand it over to Kimberly.

"Kimberly, write this down," I said.

"You're the recorder," she replied.

"I *was* the recorder."

She reluctantly grabbed the paper and pencil as I dictated.

"It's heavier than I predicted. It rolls, and then hits something and stops rolling. No, there are two rolling balls in here."

"Let me see," Kimberly reached for the box.

"Only if you promise to share every box with me."

"I promise," she said reluctantly.

I handed her the box and she agreed with my findings. "Yeah, definitely two balls, at least. Maybe three?"

I took back the paper and finished writing down the observations while Mrs. Cooper counted, "One, two, three," and we passed the boxes clockwise to the next table.

At the end of class we were allowed to look inside the boxes to see if our observations were correct.

The box that we were sure held two balls had two billiard balls in it. That's why it was so heavy.

And the first box, which I never got the chance to hold, held a pawn from a chess set.

"OK class, no homework today," said Mrs. Cooper as she was dismissing us. "When you come back tomorrow, remember to sit in these same seats."

Ugh! Same seats? Tomorrow? This most definitely would not do. I went to talk to Mrs. Cooper about my seat, but Kimberly got to her first. I was certain she was saying something bad about me.

5

(Don't) Break a Leg

I would have thought that an hour of PE, walking around the track over and over again, would have gotten Kimberly Newhouse out of my head. I would have thought that. But I'd be wrong. In fact, the opposite was true. Walking around the track gave me more time to ruminate about all the possible ways I could get even with her. So much so, that I was terribly worked up by the time I got to my locker.

Luckily, Andrea was there waiting for me.

"Well, how was your first class with the 'Teacher of the Year?'"

"Don't get me started," I exclaimed as I angrily dialed my locker code. The code didn't work. "You wouldn't believe it if I told you!"

"Try me," Andrea said.

I dialed the code again as I told Andrea how I was forced to not only sit next to Kimberly Newhouse, but that she was going to be my lab partner for the entire unit!

"How long does a unit last?" Andrea asked.

"I don't know!" I slammed on my locker after the second time I failed to unlock it. "With my luck, probably the whole year!"

"Here, let me," said Andrea, opening my locker door for me. We both knew each other's locker combination by heart.

"Don't you think you're exaggerating a little?" she asked as she opened the locker door. "Besides, can't you talk to Mrs. Cooper and ask to change partners?"

I wasn't in the mood for reason. I wanted to vent. But Andrea wasn't having any of it this afternoon. I admitted that I had tried to talk to her after school, but that Kimberly got there first.

"I'll talk to her tomorrow before fifth period, which means I may miss you at lunch."

We walked outside to the front of the school and watched as two men on exceedingly high ladders hung up a banner that read 'Welcome Back Taft Tigers, Congratulations to Our Teacher of the Year!'"

"I guess that makes it official," Andrea said, reading the sign out loud.

So far, I was not convinced. I started walking to my mom's office, but Andrea held back.

"Aren't you coming?" I asked.

"You don't remember?" she asked.

"Remember what?"

"My audition!"

"Oh my goodness," I exclaimed. "I got so worked up over science class that I completely forgot!"

"That's OK. I forgive you," Andrea said smiling. "But I am terribly nervous. I can feel my heart beating in my throat."

"Do you want me to wait for you?" I asked.

"Nah, it'll be a while. Besides, remember that we're going to the IMAX afterschool tomorrow."

"How could I forget?" I replied, though clearly, I wouldn't put it past me to forget anything today.

I told Andrea to break a leg - apparently, you're not supposed to wish a singer 'Good luck!' I had made that mistake the year before. To save you the gory details, I will not divulge what happened in these pages.

My mom worked at the Museum of Natural History which had an IMAX with a 7-story screen. I got to see as many movies there as I wanted.

Andrea and I parted ways, she to her audition, and me to my mom's office.

6

Parents Just Don't Get It

The museum was about a mile straight down University Blvd. It was so close we would walk there whenever we went for field trips.

I had so looked forward to 8th grade, I thought to myself as I walked. I remember how big the 8th graders looked when I entered Taft two years ago. They seemed to have all their stuff together. They were confident. They were mature. And here I was, my first day in 8th grade, and I was none of these things. Yes, I was beginning to hate 8th grade.

I passed the ice cream store. That was where the popular kids hung out after school. I always made sure to walk on the opposite side of the street so as not to run into them.

Sure enough, there was Kimberly Newhouse, along with David Henry and Trish Cunningham, sitting at a table in front. They were surrounded by at least four others, standing around them.

Gosh she made me so mad!

I wish she'd just ignore me like the other popular girls. Not Kimberly. She noticed me all right, enough to hurl insults at me. And her friends would laugh along with her. I could feel them talking about me as I walked past the shop. I pretended not to notice. I picked up my pace.

I ducked into the coffee shop down the block and ordered my usual, double frozen mocha with whipped cream.

By the time I had reached the museum, I had already finished half of it.

"Hi Leticia," I greeted the security guard as I walked through the employee entrance.

"How was the first day of school?" she asked me. Her son James was in my class, but we weren't close.

"What could you expect? It's school, after all," I responded, opting for small talk at the moment. If Leticia really wanted to know how my first day was, she'd have to bring in the psychiatrist's couch, and sit for a while. A LONG while.

I took the stairs up to the third floor and walked into my mom's office. To my disappointment, she wasn't there. I plopped myself into her desk chair and waited, burying my problems into the last few slurps of my double frozen mocha... with whipped cream.

I had barely finished when my mom entered carrying a dead animal's skull.

"Look who the cat dragged in," she exclaimed, with that big mom smile that usually makes me feel all warm inside. Today it didn't. "Well, how was your first day?"

"Miserable!" I responded.

"Why? What happened?" she asked, putting the skull down on a table and walking over to me.

"I hate eighth grade!" I remarked again. "And Mrs. Cooper's class was the worst!"

"Mrs. Cooper? You've been eager to take her class for two years! Tell me what happened," my mom asked, sitting down across from me.

"She teamed me up with Kimberly Newhouse of all people! She makes me so mad!"

"Mrs. Cooper?"

"No, Kimberly Newhouse! Haven't you been listening!" I accused my mom.

"I'm trying to. Continue," she said.

"She seated me next to Kimberly Newhouse. And we were forced to work together. And she wouldn't even let me have a try at the activity. She's the worst!"

"What happened between you and Kimberly?" my mom asked. "You two used to be the best of friends. I remember how you two would spend hours together playing video games up in your room."

"As soon as she became popular, she turned into a witch!" I exclaimed.

"Come on, she couldn't be that bad."

"She called me a geek!"

"Now catch me up. A 'geek' is a bad thing? Because I recall when being a computer geek was a good thing."

"Mom, get it together!" My impatience was growing. "Geek has never been a good thing! When you're in middle school, you don't want to be different. You just want to fit in."

"There'll be a time Sam when you'll be glad you don't."

"You always say that," I said.

"I say it because it's true."

There were times my mom frustrated me so much and this was one of those times. She just didn't get it. She knew nothing of what it's like to be a middle-schooler. Hadn't she been a middle-schooler once in her life?

"Anyway, forget about Kimberly. Tell me about science class. What did you learn?"

"Nothing," I responded. By this time, I just wanted the conversation to end.

"I'm sure you learned something," she said.

"No really, nothing. We learned nothing. We passed around boxes that had stuff in it and we had to figure out what was inside. And I barely got a chance to even do that." I started looking up RFID tags on my mom's computer to see if I could troubleshoot Einstein's collar device. "When are we going to get to science?" I asked.

"Well, I'd trust Mrs. Cooper if I were you," my mom said. "Students rave about her class - you told me yourself. Besides, you don't get to be 'Teacher of the Year' for nothing."

Teacher of the year. Yep. Big deal. I said dismissively to myself, as I continued to look stuff up on the computer.

"What homework do you have?" my mom continued.

"Mom, they don't give homework on the first day."

"Good, then you can help me here."

I loved helping my mom at the museum. And maybe that would keep my mind off my horrible day.

7

Foiled Again!

W The next day I reminded Andrea at the beginning of school that I was going to talk to Mrs. Cooper at lunch. As we were going to the IMAX together after school anyway, she was cool to spend lunch with Freddy and Deon, though they weren't much company to be honest. They didn't talk much, and when they did, they mainly spoke about their super-geeky Dungeons and Dragons obsession.

At the end of fourth period, I packed up my stuff quickly and was one of the first people out the door at the lunch bell. I hurried across the quad to Mrs. Cooper's classroom to make sure I would catch her before she left for the teachers' lounge. Luckily, her door was still open. I walked in and was shocked to see her talking with Kimberly Newhouse. Again! What was Kimberly doing there? And how in the world did she get to Mrs. Cooper before me?

They continued doing what they were doing when I entered the room, not even noticing me. What were they so focused on?

Mrs. Cooper got up from her seat, saw me and said, "Have a seat. I'll be with you in a few minutes." Kimberly, who had her back to me the whole time, turned around to see who Mrs. Cooper was talking to. She smirked at me. And then turned back around. I was so embarrassed. Do I stay and wait? I wanted so desperately to run out of there, but how could I do that after Mrs. Cooper already saw me?

All these questions were running through my mind as Mrs. Cooper retrieved a rack of test tubes from the back room.

"You generally don't want to be carrying test tubes in their trays, but rather bring the trays to the students and then hand out the test tubes separately," I overheard her explain to Kimberly. "But in the interest of time, let me show you what I want in each setup."

Mrs. Cooper paused, deep in thought.

"You know what, let's go to the back room and I'll show you around," she eventually added.

On the way to the back room, Mrs. Cooper looked over at me one more time. "We won't be long." Kimberly smirked at me again.

Ugh! The door to the back room closed behind them. On it read a sign:

Keep Out!
Authorized Personnel Only
Do Not Clean

This was my opportunity to escape. Clearly this was the worst time possible to talk to Mrs. Cooper, and to think that she brought Kimberly to the back room with her? Students were never allowed in the back where they stored chemicals! How did Kimberly get special dispensation? And a tour on top of that?

She must be training Kimberly to be her lab tech! There was no other explanation. That was the position that I had wanted ever since I was a little kid — or at least a sixth grader! Kimberly double-crossed me again. And what did she do to deserve it?

Science was *my* thing, not hers. When I would dig up worms out of the backyard to look at under the microscope, she would have absolutely nothing to do with it. Kimberly had absolutely zero interest in science. So why was she chosen as Mrs. Cooper's lab tech? What did Mrs. Cooper see in her?

I ran out of the room while I had the chance and flung myself headfirst into Mr. Phillips, the school principal.

"There, there, Ms. Gold, watch where you're going. And no running in the halls!" He yelled after me, as I did the fastest run-walk my legs would muster. *See, I'm not running!* I could barely hold it together as I made my way to the cafeteria to find Andrea. It was harder and harder to hold back tears, but I didn't want any of the other kids to see me cry.

As soon as I reached the cafeteria the bell rang. Instead of finding my best friend, I nearly got trampled by the seemingly hundreds of students piling out of the cafeteria on their way to fifth period. After getting my bearings I looked in the sea of people for Andrea, but I couldn't find her. I wasn't even sure she had eaten her lunch there today. I really needed to find her. How was I going to be able to sit through fifth period science without her help? And yet, as the sea of students diminished to a trickle, there was no sign of her. And I of course, had to go to class.

I walked slowly to fifth period, hoping that I'd be picked up by the security guard or even better Mr. Phillips. Detention suddenly seemed like a far better option. Unfortunately for me, I wasn't even noticed as I dragged my way down the quad to the science building, and to Mrs. Cooper's class. I looked inside the window before I entered, and there was Kimberly Newhouse at the lab table, with her things spread out over where I was supposed to sit. Feeling sick to my stomach, yet unfortunately not sick enough to see the nurse, I steadied myself, dried any tears that were still lingering on my eyelashes, and made my best attempt at walking proudly into Mrs. Cooper's class.

Mrs. Cooper looked at me and then glanced over to the wall clock. She didn't say anything, yet I got the message loud and clear.

I sat next to Kimberly and shoved her things toward her as I made room for my own backpack. I was not going to let her win.

8

It's What's Inside That Counts

"Yesterday, class, we looked at how scientists can use their senses to observe phenomena they cannot see," Mrs. Cooper began. "Just because something cannot be seen by the human eye does not mean it doesn't exist. Take this classroom. There are approximately 1×10^{28} air molecules in this room, mostly nitrogen, oxygen, and carbon dioxide molecules. That's 10," she said, walking over to the white board, "with 28 zeroes." She drew all 28 zeroes.

"Which is 10 octillion," she said, turning around to face us.

"Or ten million billion trillion molecules.

"That's a difficult number to comprehend. Let me put it in terms you can relate to. Who here likes money?"

Everyone raises their hand.

"Let's say you were an octillionaire. If you had octillion one-dollar bills, your wealth would cover the surface of planet earth, 9 miles high. 9 miles. That's higher than Mt. Everest."

"You could buy a lot of things with a Mt. Everest stack of dollar bills," she continued.

"Simon, you could buy that VR headset you've been saving for," one of the boys called out.

"Simon could buy a lifetime supply of disposable VR headsets for everyone in the world," Mrs. Cooper added.

"And yet, there are more than octillion molecules in this room. One octillion dollar bills. We don't see them. But we know they're there. If they weren't, we wouldn't be able to breathe."

"So going back to yesterday's question, 'How do scientists know what they know?'"

"Thoughts?" she asked again, indicating that she wanted feedback.

Mrs. Cooper called on Allison, who always raised her hand.

"Yesterday, we couldn't see what was in the box, but we could hear it, and feel it."

"Yes, one way is to use your other senses," said Mrs. Cooper. "But what if you can't hear it or feel it? How do you know it's there?"

The class was silent. Perhaps they were thinking. I was trying ever-so-slightly to defend my space on the lab table as Kimberly's stuff was ever-so-slowly creeping onto my side.

"I know!" Kimberly spoke out. "We can use instruments that can detect things we can't."

"Yes, instruments, Kimberly. Does anyone have an example?" said Mrs. Cooper.

Not about to be out-performed by Kimberly, I said, "I use instruments such as sensors, motion sensors and light sensors, to program my Raspberry Pi."

"Yes, sensors are an example of instrumentation. I'd love to talk later about your work with the Raspberry Pi, uh..."

"Sam," I said. "Sam Gold." I smiled the big, broad smile of victory, and pushed Kimberly's stuff back toward her.

Mrs. Cooper pulled a ruler off her desk and asked, "Could a ruler ever be an instrument?" Allison raised her hand again.

"You," she pointed to another student whose hand wasn't raised.

"Who me?" he asked.

"Remind me your name," said Mrs. Cooper.

"Evan."

"Evan, could a ruler ever be an instrument?"

"I guess, maybe."

"Cool! I can replace my trumpet with a ruler," another kid chimed in. His name was Nick. And he was quite a good trumpet player. But his personality at times mimicked that of a trumpet. Blaring, noticeable and attention-getting.

"Well, in 1994 scientists at the National Research Council in Canada created the world's smallest ruler – each division measured the width of 18 atoms! It was created in order to measure features on a computer chip that were one-60th the width of a human hair. The calibrations of this ruler were so small that it made it into the Guinness Book of World Records. In 1911, 80 years earlier, Ernest Rutherford and his colleagues Hans Geiger and Ernest Marsden were able to accurately measure the size of the nucleus of a single gold atom. Atoms are the particles that make up the whole universe. They make up you and me. And they make up this desk." She knocked on her desk for emphasis.

"The nucleus is the positive center of every atom. Rutherford and his team were able to measure its size without such a ruler. So let me ask again, how do you think they were able to do this?" Mrs. Cooper asked.

"Ernest Rutherford and his team designed an experiment," she continued, not waiting for an answer, "to study the atom indirectly. They used gold foil that was only a few atoms thick. And directed alpha particles at it. Alpha particles are particles with a positive charge that are given off by a sample of uranium. What do you guys know about uranium?" she asked the class.

I raised my hand. So did Allison.

"Yes, Allison?" said Mrs. Cooper.

"It's radioactive," she said.

"Exactly correct. Uranium is radioactive."

"It's dangerous," someone else said.

"Wasn't uranium used in the atomic bomb?" asked Nick.

"Yes, uranium was used in the first atomic bomb," Mrs. Cooper acknowledged.

"But plutonium was used in the second," I chimed in. If Nick wasn't waiting to be called on, I wasn't going to wait either.

"Yes, Sam, you are correct," Mrs. Cooper acknowledged.

"Uranium — just like plutonium — is radioactive. Which means particles leak out of the atom's nucleus. Some of these particles are positively-charged particles called alpha particles.

"So, Rutherford and his team aimed alpha particles at the gold foil, almost like shooting bullets at it. And by watching what happened to these 'alpha particle bullets' after they hit the gold foil, they could figure out what was inside the gold foil.

"The thing was, these alpha particles moved really quickly, and were invisible, just like the atoms in the foil themselves. So, they set up a screen around the foil that would light up whenever an alpha particle hit it. They could then measure the trajectory of the alpha particle based on where it landed."

"I saw that in an NCIS episode. They could tell exactly where the shooter stood by measuring the angle the bullets went into the victim," Nick called out.

"I saw that one too," said Simon.

"So, this is similar, except these 'alpha particle bullets' were too small to see. Today, we're going to model Rutherford's experiment by rolling marbles against a target we can't see. Your task is to figure out the shape of the target, by watching how it changes the trajectory of the marbles. Let's start by handing out the 'alpha particle marbles.' Kimberly?"

Kimberly got up from her seat and started distributing a bag of marbles from Mrs. Cooper's desk. I had almost forgotten about my feud with Kimberly until Mrs. Cooper called on her. I was so angry... and jealous.

"Next, we will set up a target at each lab station. It will be covered by plywood so that you cannot see it. Do not under any circumstances lift the plywood to peer underneath."

Mrs. Cooper and Kimberly distributed the targets covered by plywood to each station. They delivered ours last, at which point Kimberly sat down again.

I had held onto the marbles waiting for our setup. We both got on the ground with the target. Kimberly reached out her hand for the marbles, but I wasn't about to hand them over.

I rolled one under the target and it came back to me angled toward the left. I picked it up and rolled again.

Kimberly grabbed a handful of marbles out of the bag and started rolling them herself.

The second time the marble went straight through to the other side, without any deflection.

"What do you think it is?" I asked Kimberly.

"I don't have a clue," I admitted.

"What if we roll all the marbles at once?" she asked.

"Try it. It couldn't hurt."

That was a mistake, as the two of us were now on our knees looking under tables, chairs and between our classmates' legs for the marbles that got away.

Clearly, we needed a better method. Or at least *a* method.

"Let's draw what's happening," I said, as I tore out a piece of lined paper from my science notebook.

I drew a square which represented the plywood cover.

"Each time we roll a marble, we should draw where it enters and where it comes out. If we do that from enough entry points, we may be able to figure out what's going on."

"I'll roll and you draw," Kimberly said.

"Oh no, you're not doing that to me again."

"Ok, you roll, and I'll draw," she offered.

"We'll take turns. I'll roll three and you draw. And then we'll switch," I said.

I was still impatient to learn about science, but I had to admit, this was sort of fun. And Kimberly, well, she was sort of fun too. It felt like we were back in elementary school when we used to spend every waking minute together.

The classroom was loud with rolling marbles and friends catching up with each other.

When it was my time to draw, Kimberly teased me for my limited drawing skills. As it turned out, she was the better drawer, and I was the better roller, so we naturally fulfilled our roles according to our strengths.

"What do you have after this?" Kimberly asked me.

"Ugh," I said. "P.E. Don't remind me."

"I hate P.E.," she said.

"No you don't. You love P.E. You're a cheerleader." I would often see her practicing cheer after school. She was far more athletic than I and hung out with the sports kids all the time.

"Why do you think I became a cheerleader?" she said. "So I could get out of P.E. Wearing those awful puke-yellow jumpsuits. You can't imagine how terrible you look in those."

"I can imagine. I see myself every day. It's awful. But you know what's worse?"

"Showering!" we both said at the same time. Then we burst out laughing. Yes, showering in front of 30 other girls was probably the worst thing you could make a middle-schooler do. My P.E. was the last period of the day. Why in the world would I need to shower there rather than in my own home, in private? It was humiliating.

"Two more minutes, then it's time to wrap up," Mrs. Cooper said over the noise.

Kimberly's drawing was nonsensical. There were a bunch of lines going in, and a bunch of lines going out. All we could figure was that there was perhaps a circular object underneath. It had to be small since most of the marbles rolled through to the other side.

"OK class," Mrs. Cooper said, calling us together. "One of you from each team, put the marbles back into the bags, and the other one, stack the plywood targets in front of my desk."

I brought the target to the front of the room. Kimberly went around collecting the marbles from every table.

As we got to our seats, Mrs. Cooper resumed, "Any thoughts on what was underneath the plywood?" she asked.

Allison raised her hand, as did I.

"Yes, Allison, go ahead."

"I think it was a circle of some sort."

"Very good. Who else thought it was a circle?" she asked. Both Kimberly and I raised our hands, as did others.

"Going back to my original question, 'How do scientists know what they know,' sometimes we as scientists have to make indirect observations, or inferences. Before Rutherford started shooting alpha particles at gold foil, he thought, as everyone did at the time, that the atom was like plum pudding."

"Plum pudding! That sounds gross," Nick said.

"Yes, well, gross or not, they thought that the atom was filled with positive stuff - that was the pudding part. And embedded in the positive pudding stuff were plums of negative charge, which they called corpuscles. We call them electrons now, not corpuscles."

Some students started saying 'corpuscles' to each other.

"As expected, when Rutherford shot alpha particles at gold foil, most of the particles went straight through. And they could tell, because the screen would light up, or scintillate, where the alpha particle would hit it. But every once in a while..." Mrs. Cooper paused for effect. "Every once in a while, an alpha particle would ricochet off the gold foil and hit the screen at an angle. And every once in a while, far less often, the alpha particle would bounce straight back to the uranium source! Rutherford exclaimed, 'It was almost as incredible as if you fired a bullet at a piece of tissue paper and it came back and hit you!' We'll talk more about what he discovered tomorrow. Today, I am assigning a group project that you and your lab partner will collaborate on that will be due next week."

Kimberly and I looked at each other at that moment.

"Your topic - the atom. You can write a song, play, build an atom, do a slide presentation, whatever you like."

Hands started going up as the bell rang. "We'll discuss this further tomorrow."

I was full of questions as I asked Kimberly, "What should we do?"

"I don't have a clue. Do you want to get together after school to work on it?" Kimberly suggested.

"Sure, but don't you have cheerleading practice?"

"Nah. The season hasn't even started. Tryouts are tomorrow."

"Oh cool. Wanna meet at our lockers?"

"Make sure you shower first," she said, laughing.

"Wouldn't miss it!" I said, as we walked out of class together before going our separate ways.

9

How to Make an Atom

I waited at the locker for Kimberly feeling grungy and gross after PE. The shower didn't help. I tried fixing myself up in the mirror to look halfway presentable. That didn't help either. I was nervous and hoping she wouldn't notice.

Andrea came by.

"Thank God we're going to the IMAX," she said. "It was the only thing getting me through the day."

Oh no! I completely forgot about our plans.

"Before we go, I need you to check the callback list with me. I'm afraid to do it alone."

I didn't know what to say.

"What's wrong?" Andrea said.

"I, uh, don't know how to tell you this."

"Hey Sam, you ready?" said Kimberly, as she opened her locker.

Andrea gave me a look that could kill.

"I, uh, Andrea, I'm so sorry. I completely forgot about our plans."

"Are you kidding me?" she said, clearly upset.

"Yeah, uh, Mrs. Cooper gave us a group assignment, and well, Kimberly and I need to work on it today."

"But WE had plans today." Andrea said.

"I know, I know. But Kimberly couldn't do tomorrow because of cheerleader tryouts." I threw that in. Though it was true, it wasn't the reason we made plans for today. Honestly, I totally forgot about Andrea and our plans to see the new IMAX.

"Tell you what, why don't you come with us!" I said.

Andrea got so mad that she just stormed off. I felt absolutely terrible. I was about to run after her when Kimberly asked, "What's her problem?

"I, uh, I completely forgot about our plans. Let me go talk to her."

I ran off after Andrea, calling at her, "Andrea, wait, stop!" But Andrea either didn't hear me or didn't want to hear me. I couldn't leave Kimberly waiting either. I didn't know what to do, but I'd make it up to Andrea somehow.

I returned to the lockers. Kimberly had folded her arms as if she were tired of waiting for me.

"I'll call her later," I said. "Let's go."

With that, we left school and started walking toward the museum.

"Have you given any thought to our project?" Kimberly asked me along our walk. I was still thinking about Andrea.

"No," I said. "Have you?"

"Yeah. I was thinking about making an atomic model, like out of styrofoam balls and stuff."

"Yeah, that would be cool. Though it reminds me of last year's astronomy project!" We had made the perfunctory solar systems out of sytrofoam balls last year with all eight planets circling the sun. It was fun and I learned a bunch, but it was so basic, my baby brother could have done it.

"Let's stop at Pete's on the way." Pete's Ice Cream was the shop I would see Kimberly and the other popular girls hanging out at as I walked to my mom's. I was so used to avoiding it by walking quickly past it, that it had never occurred to me to be a destination. But hey, I was with the most popular girl in school, so why not?

"Sure," I said. Of course, I was looking forward to my mocha on the way, but when in Rome...

As we walked into the shop, Kimberly was greeted by everyone, including the employees, as if she owned the place. "Hey Carl, Nina!" she said to two of her friends.

"Where's David?" Carl asked.

"He had to stay after school for practice," Kimberly answered, as she walked to the counter and ordered her 'usual.'

I wasn't sure what to order, but feeling awkward and out of place and desperately wanting to fit in, I added, "I'll have the same."

As I watched them prepare the 'usual,' I was relieved that the guy started scooping from the mint chocolate chip ice cream tub. Soon enough I learned that the 'usual' was a mint chocolate shake with whipped cream, chocolate shavings and a cherry on top.

We took our shakes to go, and I waited at the curb as Kimberly checked in with more friends, some of the conversations taking longer than I had hoped. I started drinking my shake. It was perfect. I could do this again. But it still felt weird being there. Especially without Andrea. I hoped again that she wasn't too mad at me. And I started thinking about how I was going to make it up to her.

Kimberly finally extricated herself from the ice cream shop and we continued to the museum. I had finished my shake by then.

"What else is there to do a project on then, if we don't make an atomic model?" Kimberly asked.

"I'm thinking that we do something that I can program with the Raspberry Pi, like real orbiting electrons."

"Do you know how to do that?"

"No," I admitted.

The entrance to the museum was just up the block.

"But, I'm sure I could figure it out," I said.

10

Is There Such a Thing as Too Much Uranium?

Kimberly knew the way to my mom's office almost as well as I did. For years, we used to walk home from school together.

"Hi Leticia," I greeted the security guard at the front. "Good afternoon Sam. Hi Kimberly, nice to see you!"

"Thanks Leticia," Kimberly said.

"How was school today?" Leticia asked me, emphasizing the word 'today' as if there was something I needed to tell her about Kimberly's sudden reappearance in my life. Leticia was one of those people that could sense what was going on without ever having to be told. This trait was ideal in a security guard. She may have under different circumstances become an excellent sleuth, or even psychologist. I can't count how many times she helped me work through my problems.

As we opened the door to the stairwell, I looked back at her and saw her giving me that all-knowing look.

We walked up to the third floor where my mom's office was. She was on the phone when we entered. "Hi Mom!" I greeted her. She gave me a broad smile and held up her finger to wait until she was off the phone.

"No, I didn't order 6 megagrams of uranium. I ordered 6 micrograms! No wonder it's being held up at the Department of the Interior. My goodness! What they must think of me! Ok, let me know. Bye bye," she said as she hung up the phone.

"Can you believe it? The museum made a mistake and ordered megagrams instead of micrograms! I'm sure the government has me listed me as public enemy number one by now. Hi honey. Kimberly, it's so good to see you," she said.

"Thank you, Dr. Gold."

"What's the difference between megagrams and micrograms?" I asked.

"A megagram is a million grams. A microgram is a millionth of one gram. All I wanted was a millionth of a gram for our new natural radiation exhibit."

"Anyway, it'll all get sorted out," my mom sad. "Kimberly, how long has it been? A year? Two years? How are your parents?"

"They're good," Kimberly said.

"So, what are you two up to?" my mom asked.

"We need to come up with an atom project. It's due next week so we wanted to get a jump on it," I explained.

"Hmm," she said. "So, what are your thoughts?"

"I wanted to make a model of the atom with styrofoam balls," Kimberly said.

"And I wanted to do something with the Raspberry Pi that would cause real-life electrons to orbit on the outside. Though, not really real-life. But you know what I mean."

"They both sound like good possibilities. Is that the assignment, to make a model of the atom?"

"We're not really sure," I explained. "Mrs. Cooper didn't have time to go much into it today. But today we learned about the gold-foil experiment. And how sometimes you can't always observe something directly, but by how it behaves."

"Interesting," my mom said.

"So, what do you think Dr. Gold?" Kimberly asked her as she sat down in one of the empty chairs.

"There are so many possibilities," she responded, seemingly deep in thought.

This was my mother's way of helping. I liked to call it not helping. She never gives a straight answer, hoping I'll come up with the answer myself. It drives me crazy! This is why my dad is far easier to go to for help. But, alas, his knowledge of science is severely limited.

"What do you think?" I asked her directly.

"Funny," she said. "I just got off the phone with procurement. They by accident ordered a huge piece of uranium for our new exhibit."

"That's the stuff that Rutherford used in his experiment," Kimberly commented.

"Yes.

"Yes. And it got me thinking, why not do a project about radioactivity, about how elements can change from one form to another?"

"What do you mean, Mom?"

"There were these people called alchemists in the Middle Ages who were trying to change lead into gold, because gold was much more valuable. Some very famous people were alchemists, like Isaac Newton..."

"The guy who got hit by a falling apple!" Kimberly interjected.

"Yes, the guy who came up with our Law of Gravity," my mom said. "But they never were able to achieve this transformation because the nucleus determines an atom's identity. It's only in the 20th century that we were able to break inside the nucleus."

"The nucleus is the positive center of the atom. We learned about that today," I said. "So, you're saying we can turn lead into gold?"

"Boy, that would be a great project!" Kimberly added.

My mom laughed. "Not too fast. First, you'd need a particle accelerator. And that's a little outside of your budget. It's even outside of the museum's budget."

"Geez," Kimberly said. "Thanks for getting our hopes up."

"But I was thinking, maybe you could do a project about how radioactivity works, and about the particles that leak out of an atom, turning one kind of atom into another."

"I don't know Mom, sounds a little boring. Where are the lights, sensors... the things I can program?" I asked.

"That's your department Sam, not mine."

"It does sound kind of interesting," Kimberly said to me. "What do you think?"

"I'm not convinced," I said.

"Well, I'm sure whatever you two come up with will be great," my mom said. "I have to get back to work and make sure I'm not being sent 6 megagrams of uranium or being arrested for ordering it in the first place."

"Do you want to walk around the museum?" I asked Kimberly.

"Sure," she said.

We left my mom to her business and walked downstairs to the main floor of the museum. We looked around at fossils, at full-scale dinosaur skeletons, and even tried out the virtual reality flight experience. Soon enough, I got tired of walking around and suggested the IMAX to Kimberly. She agreed.

As usual, we were let in without a ticket, got our 3D glasses and found seats toward the back center of the theater.

"What do you think of doing a report on radioactivity?" I asked Kimberly.

"I'd prefer not doing too much writing," she said.

"Yeah, me too," I agreed, as I watched people enter the theater, hoping that no one would take the seat right next to me. Usually, the theater was pretty empty during school days.

"Unless we made a model of a radioactive atom, like the uranium your mom was talking about."

"We could have it change its identity by giving off radioactive particles," I added.

"Yeah!" Kimberly said.

"And I'm sure I could program that somehow with the Raspberry Pi. But then again, we only have a week to do it."

"Do you think you could get it done in time?"

"Yeah, I think I could," I said as I started thinking about all the possibilities of programming a radioactive atom.

With that, the movie started, so we put on our 3D glasses, and I sank into my seat. It was good to be with Kimberly again. Gosh how I had missed her.

11

Brownies Fix Everything

My mom drove us home after the movie and we agreed to meet up again after school tomorrow to get started on building our radioactive atom.

After we dropped Kimberly off, I told my mom how I had let Andrea down, and that she was not answering any of my texts.

My mom suggested we make brownies to bring to school tomorrow as part of an apology.

Andrea loved brownies. Who wouldn't? I thought that was a good idea, so we set out to bake them after dinner.

The next morning, I crafted a note to attach to the brownies:

I'm so sorry.
Please forgive me.
- Your BFF Sam

"Sam! Your stupid machine didn't work! Einstein peed in the house again!"

Just once I'd like to have a morning without having to hear my annoying little brother.

I packed my backpack, grabbed the note, and ran downstairs. I wanted to make sure to get to our meetup spot early so I wouldn't miss Andrea.

"Alex, I need you to do me a huge favor," I told my brother, who was taking 'crime scene' photos of Einstein's mess.

"I'm not cleaning it up. Uh-uh. No way," he said.

"Just this one time. I have to run to school."

"Nope." Alex said.

"What do you want?"

"Your brownies."

"Anything but the brownies," I said, picking them up and attaching the note to the box with some scotch tape."

"The brownies, or no deal."

"I'll give you one brownie."

"No deal."

"Two. That's my final offer. They're for Andrea."

"Three," he said.

I looked inside the box. I made her 12. I figured 9 would say "I'm sorry" nearly as much as 12.

"Deal." I put the box back on the table, took out 3 of the worst-looking brownies in the bunch and put them on a plate.

"Aren't you eating breakfast?" My father asked.

"Not today Dad, I'm late."

"Thanks Alex!" I said, packing up the box, and running out the door.

I was right on time to our spot, though I had planned to be early. Andrea would be coming by any minute. I waited. After a few minutes had gone by, I texted her.

I waited for a response.

And waited.

No answer.

Alex walked by, with brownie crumbs on his mouth and a huge grin.

"You might want to wipe your mouth before anyone sees you."

He rubbed his mouth against his sleeve and said, "I was just saving that for later."

"Where's Andrea?" he asked.

I didn't like him butting into my business.

"Do you want me to wait with you?" he asked, in his smarmy little brother style.

"No. I. Don't. Go or you'll be late to school."

"Not any more than you," he said, still facing me, walking backwards toward school.

After he disappeared, I texted Andrea again:

I waited for an answer.

Still nothing.

One thing Alex was right about was that I was going to be late to school. Tardies didn't mean nearly as much to me as getting back on Andrea's good side. But too many tardies and I'd get detention which was a major inconvenience. Besides, I'd probably find Andrea at her locker. After all, maybe her phone was dead. Or she left it at home.

I hurried onto school, looking back every half a block or so to see if Andrea appeared behind me.

There was no sign of her, so I quickened the pace and made it to her locker just as the first bell rang.

I must have just missed her. Students were running to class and I needed to get a move on too. I dialed her locker combination and opened the door. Inside the door was a pic I had printed out of the two of us last year in our Halloween costumes Laverne and Shirley. It made me smile. I left the brownies with the note.

And hurried on to first period, American History.

12

As If Things Couldn't Get Worse

I was so anxious to get to the cafeteria to see Andrea, that I quietly packed my things in English class early. I wanted to be first out the door. But Mrs. McCabe kept droning on and on about the onomatopoeia in Edgar Allen Poe's "The Raven":

While I nodded, nearly napping, suddenly there came a tapping,
As of some one gently rapping, rapping at my chamber door.

I actually was a huge fan of Poe. My dad used to read to me "El Dorado" before bed, and I'd go to bed dreaming of cities of gold.

But now was not the time. Why couldn't she let us out early just this once?

While I nodded, nearly napping, suddenly there came a tapping...

Everything was in my backpack ready to go by the time the bell finally rang.

"Sam, may I see you for a moment?" asked Mrs. McCabe, as I lurched out of my seat toward the door.

Darn! Not only might I miss Andrea, but now I was now in trouble. Could this day get any worse?

I waited for Mrs. McCabe as she finished conversations with other students, and then got around to me.

"Sam, is something the matter?" she asked.

"The matter?" I repeated. "No, everything's fine."

"You appear to lack focus today."

Mrs. McCabe had been my sixth grade English teacher too, so she knew me pretty well.

"Oh no, I'm sorry. I just, uh, didn't get a lot of sleep last night," I said, faking a yawn. I didn't lack focus, I thought to myself. I am extremely focused on talking to Andrea.

"Ok well, make sure you get to sleep early tonight," she said.

"I'll be sure of that," I said. "Can I go?"

"Yes."

"Thanks Mrs. McCabe," I said and walked out of the room.

Darn. Darn. Darn. Darn. If I miss Andrea because of Mrs. McCabe... I thought to myself. The lines into the cafeteria had already started to shrink by the time I got there. I snuck through the students waiting in the line to get inside. The last thing I was thinking about was food.

Past the throngs of students, I saw Andrea at our table, along with Deon and Freddy as usual. The box of brownies was at the table, unopened.

I rushed to the table.

"I'm so sorry, Rach," I said.

"No, I'm sorry Sam. I overreacted," Andrea said.

"No, I should've never canceled our plans."

"Especially for Kimberly Newhouse," Andrea agreed.

"Yes, especially for Kimberly Newhouse," I said.

"What do you see in her anyway?" Andrea asked. "She's so superficial."

"She was different in elementary school. But then she got popular and dumped me like a hot potato. Anyway, we have to do this science project together. As soon as it's done, it'll be 'Bye, bye, Kimberly'."

"Buh-bye Kimberly," Andrea repeated.

"No way," Freddy said.

"What?" I asked Freddy.

"You'd do anything for Kimberly," Freddy said.

"Nu-uh," I said. "Maybe that was true years ago."

"Well, we'll see," Freddy added. It floored me how prescient Freddy was, and how it rang true. I would have done anything for Kimberly. And despite how she's treated me, it felt so good to spend the afternoon with her yesterday. It was like old times.

"Ignore him," I said to Andrea.

"Already done," Andrea said. "Brownie?" she offered me, opening the box.

We each took one and ate it. The brownie reminded me that I hadn't eaten yet today. All this worry over Andrea had caused me to skip two meals.

Deon and Freddy were looking on, drooling over the brownies.

Andrea reluctantly offered each of them a brownie as well, "Ok, but just one."

"Guess what?" Andrea said as they were chewing on their brownies. "I got a call back from my audition!"

"Was there any doubt?" I remarked.

"Yass. Totally." Andrea said.

"Nah. You're a shoo-in! I'm so happy for you! When are the call-backs?"

"Next Monday after school."

"You'll do great," Sam said. "Break a leg!"

"Can we go see the IMAX after school today?" Andrea asked.

I felt guilty about having already seen the new film with Kimberly, so I didn't fess up.

"Can we tomorrow? I have to work on our project today," I said, trying carefully to surgically remove any mention of Kimberly from my reply.

From the look on Andrea's face, I could tell I didn't make a clean cut.

"Again? You're spending time with her two days in a row?"

I could feel Andrea getting angry all over again.

Deon and Freddy quietly picked up their trays and left. They could sense an eruption was about to take place and they didn't want to have any part of it.

"It's just this week. For the project. I don't have a choice."

It's true. I didn't have a choice. I didn't choose to be partnered with Kimberly. Yes, I was trying to make the best of it. And I sort of actually enjoyed spending time with her. But the last thing I wanted was to upset Andrea.

"We'll go tomorrow, just the two of us," I promised her.

"We better," she said.

The bell rang and I walked with Andrea as she emptied her tray so that we could leave the cafeteria together.

"I've got P.E. now," she said.

"Ugh," I remarked. "Well, break a leg," I said.

"Don't tell me to break a leg in P.E.! That's the worst thing you could say," Andrea said as we parted.

You ever have one of those days where everything you say and do is wrong? I was getting the sense that I should have never gotten out of bed. But, it was too late for that, as I hurried across the quad to Mrs. Cooper's class.

13

The Uranium Goes Missing

Kimberly was already seated at our lab desk by the time I got to class. I was glad to see her.

"Hey," I said as I sat down next to her.

"Hi," she said. "Did you figure out how to program our radioactive atom?"

"I'm still working on it." The truth was, I hadn't thought much about our actual project since before the IMAX yesterday. I had been so tied up in knots over Andrea.

"Well, you'll have extra time because I forgot all about cheerleading tryouts after school today," she said.

"So you're not coming with me after school?" I asked.

"Good afternoon class," Mrs. Cooper began.

"I completely forgot," Kimberly whispered. "Can we do tomorrow instead?"

I felt a rush of disappointment well up inside of me.

"Yesterday we talked about Rutherford's gold foil experiment," said Mrs. Cooper, addressing the class. "Who can tell me the significance of that?"

I was looking forward to us hanging out at the museum again today. And I'd already upset Andrea about it. I couldn't cancel on her again.

"He figured out what was inside the atom using indirect evidence," a student said.

"I... don't know," I whispered back.

"Ladies," Mrs. Cooper said to us, "could you finish up your private conversation on your own time?"

We stopped talking immediately. It was embarrassing to be called out by Mrs. Cooper.

"Rutherford, using uranium as a source of alpha particles, shot them at gold foil and some of the alpha particles ricocheted straight back at him," Mrs. Cooper continued. "What was happening?"

Allison raised her hand again.

Mrs. Cooper called on Diego.

"Maybe the alpha particles hit something in the gold foil that caused them to bounce back," Diego said.

"Exactly, Diego. They hit something and bounced back. So, what did they hit?"

Allison raised her hand again, but Mrs. Cooper continued.

"Remember I told you that alpha particles have a positive charge. And opposite charges attract. But like charges repel each other." Mrs. Cooper paused to make sure the class was comprehending.

"For the alpha particle to be repelled by something in the gold foil," she continued, "what charge would that something in the gold foil have to have?

"Yes, Allison." Allison had kept her hand up since the last question.

"Positive!" Allison answered.

"You're absolutely correct. For the alpha particle to be repelled by the gold foil, to ricochet off of it, the gold foil would have had to have a positive charge too. But, since the alpha particles went through the gold foil most of the time, the positive charged things in the gold foil couldn't have been everywhere, but only in certain places.

"What Rutherford discovered," she continued, as she proceeded to draw a diagram on the white board, "was the nucleus, which was the tiny part of each atom that contained all its positive charge, all of the protons.

"And it's the number of protons in the nucleus that determines the identity of the atom."

"When you look for gold on the periodic table, it's symbol is Au," Mrs. Cooper pointed toward the huge periodic table on her wall, "What number is it?"

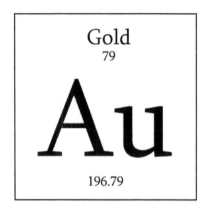

There were a lot of numbers on the chart, so I wasn't sure what she was asking. Someone called out "79."

"Yes, 79. That means, a nucleus with 79 protons will always be gold. If the nucleus only had 78 protons, what would it be?

I raised my hand but wasn't called on.

Someone else answered, "Platinum."

"Correct, Platinum. Now, if gold lost one of its protons, it would become platinum. And, if lead... Here's lead on the table," she pointed at Pb. "Lead has how many protons?"

5B	6B	7B		8B		1B	2B	Aluminum 3▪9E2	Silicon 29.84	Phosphorus 474▪	
23 V Vanadium 5▪9▪2	24 Cr Chlorium 51.41	25 Mn Manganese 5498	26 Fe Iron 55.843	27 Co Cobalt 5▪6▪	28 Ni Nickel 5▪44	29 Cu Cooper 53.86	30 Zn Zinc ▪5.38	31 Ga Gallium 6▪.72	32 Ge Germanium 72.43	33 As Arsenic 74.42	34 Se
41 Nb Niobium 92.906	42 Mo Molybdenum 95.94	43 Tc Technetium 98.9062	44 Ru Ruthenium 101.07	45 Rh Rhodium 102.9	46 Pd Palladium 106.4	47 Ag Silver 107.87	48 Cd Cadmium 112.41	49 In Indium 114.82	50 Sn Tin 118.71	51 Sb Antimony 121.75	52 T
73 Ta Tantalum 180.94	74 W Tungsten 183.84	75 Re Rhenium 186.21	76 Os Osmium 190.23	77 Ir Iridium 192.22	78 Pt Platinum 195.08	79 Au Gold 196.97	80 Hg Mercury 200.59	81 Tl Thallium 204.38	82 Pb Lead 207.2	83 Bi Bismuth 208.98	84 P
105 Db Dubnium 262	106 Sg Seaborgium 266	107 Bh Bohrium 264	108 Hs Hassium 269	109 Mt Meitnerium 268	110 Ds Darmstadtium 281	111 Rg Roentgenium 272	112 Cn Copernicium 285	113 Uut Ununtrium 286	114 Fl Flerovium 289	115 Uup Ununpentium 289	116 L

A few students simultaneously called out "82."

"Yes, if lead, which has 82 protons, suddenly lost 3 of those protons, what would it be?"

I raised my hand. I knew this one. My mom was just talking about it yesterday.

"Sam," Mrs. Cooper called on me.

"Gold, just like the alchemists!"

"Right you are," she said.

"Just like your name," Sarah added.

"An alpha particle, like the ones Rutherford shot at the gold foil, contains two protons. So, when an atom of uranium gives off an alpha particle, which is two protons... When uranium loses two protons, what atom does it become?"

"Peter?" she called.

"Huh?" he replied.

"Peter, pay attention. When uranium," she pointed to uranium, "loses two protons," she moved the pointer back two elements, it becomes..."

Rutherfordium (261)	Dubnium (262)	Seaborgium (266)	Bohrium (264)	Hassium (269)	Meitnerium (268)	Darmstadtium (269)
57 La Lanthanum 138.91	58 Ce Cerium 140.12	59 Pr Praseodymium 140.91	60 Nd Neodymium 144.24	61 Pm Promethium 145	62 Sm Samarium 150.36	63 Eu Euphorium 151.96	64 Gad
89 Ac Actinium 227	90 Th Thorium 232.04	91 Pa Protactinium 231.04	92 U Uranium 238.03	93 Np Neptunium 237	94 Pu Plutonium 244	95 Am Americium 243	96 C

"Thorium?" he answered.

"Right you are. Thorium. Now uranium is a naturally radioactive element, meaning it gives off alpha particles all the time. So, before our very eyes, it's turning into thorium. But not all elements do this. Just the radioactive ones. And not all radioactive atoms give off alpha particles. Some give off beta particles instead. And they all give off gamma rays, which are dangerous high energy electromagnetic radiation."

"Want to see something radioactive?" she added, after the weight of her last statement sunk in.

"No," most students said.

"Yeah!" said Nick, unable to contain his excitement. A few other students agreed with him.

I have to admit I was a little curious myself.

"Ok, well, I will show you something radioactive, but first you need to learn how to keep yourself safe.

"Whenever you're around a radioactive substance you have to protect yourself from exposure," she continued. "The truth is, you're being exposed to radioactivity all the time. After all, there's natural radioactivity all around us. There are even radioactive atoms in your own body."

I heard some gasps in the room.

"But you can minimize the risks. Let's start with alpha particles. Remember I told you that they contain two protons. They also contain two neutrons, which don't have any charge, but weigh the same as the protons. So an alpha particle is four times the weight of a proton. As far as radioactive particles go, they're pretty heavy.

Because they're so heavy, alpha particles can cause the most damage, but they're also the easiest to protect yourself against. Just your clothes, even your skin itself, can protect yourself from these massive particles.

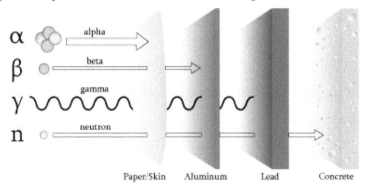

"The next type of particle, the beta particle, I haven't taught you about yet. The beta particle is the size of one electron. Now, in the world of atoms, if I were able to use a magic shrinking machine, to shrink you to the size of a proton, an electron or beta particle would still be too small to see.

"And, because it's not nearly as big as an alpha particle, it can't cause as much damage. But, because it's so small, it can reach places that alpha particles cannot. Beta particles can be stopped by a piece of plywood. Even your skin is reasonably effective at blocking beta particles, but not nearly as good at blocking alpha particles.

"Which brings me to gamma rays, which aren't particles at all. Gamma rays are a form of electromagnetic energy. Light is also a form of electromagnetic energy. The difference between visible light and gamma rays is that gamma rays are much higher energy than light. You want to protect yourself from gamma rays. They're even more damaging, more energetic, than x-rays. Gamma rays can go straight through your body.

"Whenever you get an x-ray, they protect you with a lead apron. Lead is a good shield against both x-rays and gamma-rays.

"So, there are a few ways to protect yourself, or what is called 'shield' yourself from alpha, beta and gamma radiation. Who can name one?"

"Yes Allison." Allison had her hand up almost before Mrs. Cooper asked the question.

"Lead!"

"Right you are. Lead protects you against all three. What else will shield you from the radioactivity? Kimberly?"

"Our clothing."

"Right. Our clothing can protect us against alpha particles and some beta particles. The thing is, we can't always be wearing lead aprons to protect ourselves from radiation. So there are two things to keep in mind when dealing with a radioactive substance. Distance and time of exposure."

Mrs. Cooper went to the board and wrote:

TIME DISTANCE SHIELDING

"What this means is, when dealing with radioactive substances, keep your distance, and limit the amount of time you spend around it.

"So now I'm going to bring out a piece of uranium ore, but only for a brief amount of time, and remember to stay back and keep your distance."

"Cool," said Nick. "Is it gonna blow up?"

"No Nick. That would require a chain reaction involving uranium-235. What I'm going to bring out is the rock from which uranium-238 is mined. The rock is commonly known as pitchblende."

"Do you have the other stuff? The 235 stuff?" Nick asked.

"No Nick. If I were enriching uranium in the back room to make more uranium-235, the Feds would be in here faster than you can say, 'School's out.'

"What if I don't want to see it?" Diego asked.

"I won't bring it out long enough to harm you, Diego. But if you really don't want to see it, then just wait outside the classroom, but don't go anywhere. I haven't dismissed you."

"Kimberly?" she directed.

Kimberly went to the back room and brought out what looked like a metal box and returned to her seat. A few students went to walk out of the classroom, but few actually walked out. Their curiosity got the better of them.

Mrs. Cooper put gloves on, opened the box, lifted up the piece of pitchblende and showed it the class. Just then, though, she wrinkled her brow worriedly, lifted the uranium up and down in her hand as if she were weighing it, placed it back inside its box, and dismissed the class. She called Kimberly over.

I had expected something more elaborate, a demonstration of sorts. From my vantage point, it looked to be just a rock. From the murmur among my classmates, they too were disappointed.

Kimberly walked over to return the box to the back room, but apparently Mrs. Cooper had something else in mind. It looked like she was scolding Kimberly under her breath. Wow, I didn't want to be in Kimberly's shoes. I had heard that Mrs. Cooper was strict, but she looked downright scary. From the back, I could see Kimberly shaking. What had she done? And how much trouble was she in? The other students had left the room by then, and I felt conspicuous eavesdropping on a seemingly private exchange. I walked toward the door and stepped halfway outside. I didn't want to butt in, but I didn't want to walk out on Kimberly either.

The bell had already rung by the time Kimberly ran out of the classroom in tears.

"What was it? What happened?" I asked her.

Kimberly started bawling once she was no longer in earshot of Mrs. Cooper.

"She thinks I took the uranium from out of her back room!" she blurted out through her tears.

"The uranium she showed us? She was holding it. How could she think you took it?"

"It was half the weight it was supposed to be. She's missing half of it. And she thinks I took it!"

"Did you?" I asked.

"You think I took it too?!"

"No, no. I was just asking. Well, if you didn't take it, then there's nothing to be afraid of."

"She's going to talk to the principal. I can't have this on my record. I just can't!"

"I tell you what. Let's find out who took the missing half and get it back to Mrs. Cooper. Then, she can't blame you for taking it."

"How would we do that?"

"I'm not sure. But give me time to think. Let's meet at our lockers after school to start looking."

"But I have cheerleader tryouts after school today," Kimberly said. "But you're right, this is more important."

"I'll tell you what. You go to your tryouts and I'll start looking after school today. I'll let you know what I find out."

"You'd do that for me?" she asked.

"What are lab partners for?" I said.

The tardy bell rang, and I was now late for P.E., and I hadn't yet changed into my puke yellow uniform.

Once I was convinced that Kimberly was alright, I ran off to P.E.

14

If You were a Piece of Uranium, Where Would You be?

I felt icky after P.E. I tried not to get my hair wet in the shower to no avail. Now my wet hair was flat against my head. I felt ugly. Hoping that I wouldn't run into anyone I knew was a fool's errand. It was middle school. I knew everybody.

Andrea looked to be leaving me a note in my locker when I got there.

"Hey, what's in the note?" I asked her from behind.

She jerked as if I had snuck up on her.

"Oh, nothing. I thought I wasn't going to run into you so I, well, I was trying to make plans with you for tomorrow.

"Let me read it," I said.

"It doesn't matter. You're here now," Andrea said. "Where's Kimberly Newhouse?" she asked teasingly.

"Oh, change in plans. She has cheerleader tryouts today. What are you doing now?" I asked her.

"Not going to the IMAX," she said, rubbing it in.

"I know, I know. I need to find a missing piece of uranium. Want to help me?"

"Uranium? As in, the stuff they make atomic bombs with?"

"Yeah."

"I, uh, don't know. Sounds dangerous."

"It's not that kind of uranium. It's just rock that has some uranium in it. Not the kind they make bombs from. Come help me."

"Sure, I guess." Andrea said.

I locked my locker and started walking down the hall.

"What does it look like, this rock we're looking for?" Andrea asked.

"It looks like any other rock."

"So how will we know when we find it?"

"Hmm. I hadn't thought about that. Let's start with Mrs. Cooper and find out what to look for."

When we arrived, I could see Mrs. Cooper talking with Mr. Phillips, the principal. I was worried for Kimberly. I knocked on the door as we came in, even though the door was ajar. I didn't want to intrude, but I sort of did want to.

"Excuse me Mrs. Cooper, Mr. Phillips. I don't mean to bother you."

"What is it, Sam?" Mr. Phillips said.

"I just, well, I was wondering if we could get a look at the uranium, because we were going to help look for it."

"That's very nice of you girls to want to help," Mr. Phillips said. "But you two should be spending your time on your homework. This is a matter that doesn't concern you." Mr. Phillips turned himself back toward Mrs. Cooper, as if dismissing us.

"But sir," I interrupted again. "It does concern us." I don't know how I got so bold as to contradict the principal, but the words flew out of my mouth. "Our friend Kimberly was blamed for this and I know she didn't do it."

Andrea looked at me in disbelief. I had failed to mention that our quest was on Kimberly's behalf.

Mr. Phillips turned around in his chair again, clearly annoyed.

"And how do you know that?" He asked.

"I, I just know," I said.

"Well, that's no defense now, is it?" He asked, trying to dismiss me again.

"And I can prove it!" I added.

"How can you prove it, Sam?" Mrs. Cooper asked.

"We're going to find out who took the uranium, and bring it back," I said.

"There, there girls, this doesn't concern you. Mrs. Cooper and I will handle this."

It seemed that Mrs. Cooper didn't altogether agree with the principal, because she retrieved the metal box from the back room to show us.

"Can I take a picture?" I asked her.

"Of course," she said.

Mr. Phillips looked annoyed.

"You shouldn't be putting your nose into school business, Sam," he told me as I took my phone out of my backpack.

"Distance and time of exposure," I repeated aloud as I got in, snapped a pic, and backed away.

"Mrs. Cooper smiled knowingly at me, closed the metal box, and returned it to the back room.

"Are you quite finished Sam?" Mr. Phillips asked.

"Yes Mr. Phillips! Andrea and I are on the case!"

With that, we left Mrs. Cooper's classroom, closed the door behind us, and stood outside looking at the photo, smiling as if we had just gotten away with something.

15

Where for Art Thou, Uranium?

"I can't believe you did that!" Andrea said.

"I know," I said.

"This doesn't concern you," Andrea said, mimicking Mr. Phillips's tone.

"You girls should be doing your homework," I said, adding my own impression of Mr. Phillips.

We giggled as we went out to the quad to search for the missing uranium.

Where to start, I wondered. "I guess we just look around and see if we find a rock that looks like this one," I said, emphasizing the picture on the phone.

And so we did. We looked at every rock we could, knowing that we had to keep our distance, and yet get close enough to see if it looked the same as the rock on my camera roll.

This became a gargantuan task. Who knew there were so many rocks in the quad? And they all pretty much looked like the rock in the picture. How could we tell a radioactive rock from all the other rocks? And, how could we be sure if the rock we were looking for was outside in the quad in the first place?

All these questions ran through my mind as we looked.

"Uranium, uranium, where for art thou, uranium?" I chanted as we looked under one bench and then another.

Andrea made up her own ditty:

Where, oh where has my little rock gone?
Oh where, oh where can it be?
It's a half not a whole
'Cause it went on a stroll
Oh where, oh where can it be?

The Taft Green Thumb Club was meeting in their garden as we walked inside the white fence which separated it from the rest of the quad. It was hard being inconspicuous. Actually, it was impossible.

"What are you guys doing here?" asked Phil, one of my classmates from elementary school.

"Just looking," I said.

"Looking for what?" he said.

"Not sure." I answered.

"Then how will you know when you find it?"

"Again, not sure," I said, which was the truth.

"Well, good luck with that."

"Thanks. We're gonna need it."

There were plenty of rocks in the garden. And there was no real way I could tell whether any of them was the rock we were looking for.

"Thanks guys," I said as we walked out of the garden.

We sat down on one of the benches. Most of the students had already gone home.

Clearly my plan was not well-conceived. How could we find a rock, that looks like every other rock, and how would we know when we found it?

"You didn't tell me we were looking for this rock for Kimberly," Andrea said, after a period of silence.

"If I had told you, would you have helped me?" I asked.

"Probably not."

"And aren't you having fun, sort of?"

"Sort of." Andrea said. "Still, she's been simply awful to you. And now... now it's as if you two are best friends."

"Not best friends," I assured Andrea. "You're my best friend."

"Lately, it hasn't felt like it," Andrea said. And added, "I hope Kimberly appreciates what you're doing for her."

"We may need to rethink our approach," I said.

"You think?" Andrea agreed.

I saw Kimberly coming over, still in her cheerleading uniform.

"So, how'd the tryout go?" I asked.

"Terrible," she said. "I've been so upset since fifth period that I couldn't focus. I got the whole routine wrong, and I fell on top of Ms. Novack while I was trying to do my flip. It was a total disaster! I can't imagine how she'd let me be on the team, let alone be head cheerleader."

"Ouch," I said. "Maybe it wasn't as bad as all that."

"It was worse," she said. "So, tell me what you found out."

"We don't have good news either. We spent all afternoon looking for a rock that looks like every other rock. And, even if we did find it, how would we know?" I said.

"There's just got to be a way!" she said.

"And it seemed as if we interrupted a conversation between Mrs. Cooper and Mr. Phillips about it too," Andrea added.

"Oh no. I don't know how I'm going to show my face in class tomorrow. Maybe I'll tell my mom I'm sick, so she'll let me stay home." Kimberly said.

"Nonsense," I said. "You didn't take the rock, so you have no reason to hide. We'll find it, I guarantee it!"

I hopefully sounded confident enough to convince Kimberly not to worry. I, myself, was worried.

16

The One Where They Talk about Pottery

That night at dinner my mom was telling the unfolding story of the 6 megagrams of uranium she had inadvertently ordered.

My dad had made my favorite meal, spaghetti and meatballs, with garlic bread.

The only thing not-so-ideal was watching Alex slurp up his pasta one strand at a time, splattering spaghetti sauce on his face with each slurp.

"Does he have to eat like that?" I asked.

"Like what?" Alex asked, smiling as he slurped up another strand.

"Ignore your brother," my father said.

"Alex, how about bringing it to your mouth with a fork," he said to Alex.

"So I had to go to procurement today to straighten this whole mess out," my mom continued, unswayed by Alex's antics.

"I couldn't figure out how they would go ahead and place an order for 6 megagrams. I mean, that's 6 million grams. The atomic bomb used just 64 thousand grams of uranium. Where in the world do they think they could order 6 megagrams anyway? And I can't even begin to imagine how much it would cost!"

"Mom, how much uranium is in pitchblende?" I asked.

"Pitchblende can contain more than 50% pure uranium," she said. "Why do you ask?"

"And what could happen if it got into the wrong hands?" I asked.

Alex made an explosion sound and gesture with his hands.

"Really, is it enough to make a bomb?" I asked.

"Not likely," she said, as she took a piece of garlic bread from the basket.

"First of all, pitchblende is not uranium. So you'd have to extract the uranium from the pitchblende, which would require hours of painstaking chemical reactions. Even then, you'd probably end up with just a fraction of the uranium that was inside.

"And even though all uranium is radioactive, only one isotope of uranium undergoes nuclear fission, meaning it splits into two roughly equal halves. And that isotope is rare in itself."

Alex pretended that his mother's impromptu lecture was putting him to sleep.

"Michelle, why can't we enjoy dinner like other families, talking about our day, the weather, and what's on TV tonight?" my dad asked.

"I thought that's why you married me, for the scintillating dinner conversation," my mom responded, smiling. "Would you really want us to be a normal family?"

"May I please be excused?" Alex asked.

"I thought you were interested in how bombs were made," my Mom said.

"I'm interested in explosions. All this other stuff is boring," said Alex.

"Make sure you finish your homework before getting online," my Dad said.

"Buh-bye folks," Alex said, running up the stairs.

"As I was saying before your father interrupted us," said my mother, winking at my dad, "The uranium that undergoes nuclear fission is only a small fraction of naturally occurring uranium — under 1 percent of it. So in order to make a nuclear bomb, you need to enrich the uranium, which means isolating the uranium-235 isotope."

"But how do you know... how do you know when you have it?" I asked.

"Have what honey?" My mom asked.

"How can you tell when you have uranium rock, or pitchblende? Or uranium?"

"Often you can see its yellow or orange color in the rock. In fact, in the 1920s it was commonly used as a glaze on pottery. It's no longer used as such, because we now know the danger of being exposed to too much radiation, but I'm sure there are still many homes that have this radioactive pottery."

"So, all yellow or orange rock is uranium?"

"No, no," my mom continued.

"So how do you know uranium's in a rock?"

"The easiest way is to use a Geiger counter."

"A Geiger counter?" I asked. "What's that?"

"A Geiger counter is a device that detects radiation. It won't tell you if you found uranium specifically, but it will tell you whether something is radioactive."

I knew right then that a Geiger counter is what I needed.

"How can I get one of those?" I asked.

"Why do you need it?"

My father started carrying dishes to the kitchen.

"Remember it's your night to wash dishes Sam," my Dad said.

"I'll be right there," I said.

But first I explained to my mom what had happened in science class that day and how we tried to find pitchblende in the quad but that I couldn't tell one rock from another. With a Geiger counter I could find the uranium just like people used metal detectors to find metal on the beach. Fortunately for me, from what I found out, Geiger counters were small, so I could look for uranium incognito.

"We have Geiger counters at the museum," my mom said. "I could let you borrow one for the day."

That was going to be perfect. My mom and I arranged to go early to the museum tomorrow, pick up the Geiger counter, and bring it to school with me.

I was so excited that I bounded upstairs before I remembered that I needed to wash the dishes.

I sent a quick text to Andrea before I returned downstairs.

> **Exciting news.**
>
> **Can't walk with you tomorrow.**
>
> Sam
>
> **Green light for Operation Uranium.**

I checked to see if Andrea received the message. I saw that she was in the process of texting me back. Meanwhile my father was calling after me to come back down and put the dishes in the dishwasher, so I ran back downstairs. I'd hear from Andrea soon enough anyway.

17

Operation U

Andrea was waiting for me at my locker when I got to school. I took the Geiger counter out of my backpack to show her.

"How does it work?" she asked.

"You just turn it on," I turned it on to show her, and "bring it close to something you think is radioactive."

Just then the Geiger counter started making a series of clicking beeps. Everyone around us was looking at us so I quickly switched it off.

"Oh my God," Andrea said. "Does that mean the lockers are radioactive? Is the missing uranium here?" Andrea asked in an undertone.

"I don't know," I said, "but that was scary."

"Why don't we put it away until after school," Andrea suggested.

"But what about the IMAX?" I asked her.

"Sam, we may be on the trail of an international uranium smuggling ring and you're thinking of a movie?" Andrea asked.

"Well, not when you put it that way."

Just then, Kimberly showed up with her boyfriend David.

"What's up guys?"

"We have a secret weapon," Andrea shared, nudging me to show Kimberly the Geiger counter in my hand. At the same time, Mr. Phillips walked by. The last thing I wanted was for the museum's Geiger counter to get confiscated.

"After school," I said, putting the Geiger counter behind my back, and using my eyes to indicate that I didn't want Mr. Phillips to find out.

"We'll meet back here," I continued.

"Until then, it's hush-hush with Operation U."

"Operation U?" Kimberly and Andrea both asked at the same time.

"Operation U, short for...," I looked around to be sure we were free from prying ears... 'Operation Uranium."

The bell rang and we went off to class, promising to meet up after school.

18

Shooting Particles

"Good afternoon scientists," Mrs. Cooper greeted us in class, with the familiar metal box in front of her.

"I have something really special today. Yesterday I showed you a piece of uranium rock, or pitchblende. What did you notice?"

Allison raised her hand as usual.

"You put it away so fast I couldn't see anything," Nick called out.

"Yes, I put it away quickly Nick. Next time, please raise your hand. Would you like to get a better look?"

Everyone agreed that they wanted to get a better look.

"First, discuss with your lab partner the necessary precautions you need to take."

"Do you remember Kimberly?" I asked, as I already knew the answer.

The sound of the rest of the class talking loudly made it more difficult to hear each other.

"Yeah, keep our distance and limit our exposure."

"Right," I said.

As the rest of the class was still talking, I asked her if Mrs. Cooper had said anything more to her.

"Not today," she said. "But the principal called my mom's cell phone after school. It was really embarrassing. My mom believes my story, but..."

"Class, finish up your last sentence and then give me your attention," Mrs. Cooper said.

"But she's concerned it's going to show up on my record."

I was about to say something else, but the room suddenly got quiet.

"Allison," Mrs. Cooper said, "will you remind us how to treat something that's radioactive?"

"Yes Mrs. Cooper," Allison said. "You want to limit the time you are around radioactivity and keep a safe distance."

"Good. Distance and time of exposure. So with that in mind..." Mrs. Cooper opened the metal box.

"Here it is. You can come up and take a closer look, but don't stay long. Let's start with that side of the classroom," she said as she pointed to the side opposite us.

"Come forward if you're interested in getting a better look."

Some of the braver students got up and darted toward the uranium. Most of the students stood back. Once they noticed that their classmates didn't self-destruct, the remaining students moved closer in to get a good look at it.

Then it was our turn. I went in to get a really good look at it, as did Kimberly. The picture I snapped yesterday didn't do it justice. I used this opportunity to memorize its features.

We were once again sent back to our seats as Mrs. Cooper closed the metal box again.

"One of the ways to demonstrate radioactivity is with a Geiger counter," Mrs. Cooper explained.

"I have one of those," I whispered to Kimberly.

She picked up her Geiger counter from the table and brought it near the metal box. There was a random click or two. But, once she opened the box again the clicking increased greatly, even more so as she brought the counter closer toward the uranium.

Mrs. Cooper then closed the box and turned off the Geiger counter.

"The Geiger counter picks up the beta particles and gamma rays that are given off by a radioactive substance. It helps to detect radioactivity, because after all, we cannot see it.

"The truth is, there is a way to see radioactivity, though a little indirectly. Who would you like to actually see radioactivity?" she asked the class.

All of us raised our hands.

Kimberly got up to help Mrs. Cooper with the setup at each station. She gave each table a plastic storage container with a plexiglass box and a lid inside.

I asked Kimberly if I could help, so she had me hand out gloves to each group, and wash bottles containing isopropyl alcohol.

Once we got back to our seats, Mrs. Cooper instructed us to take out our goggles from the lab drawers and to wear them throughout the rest of the experiment.

I didn't want to put mine on. The other classmates looked goofy, and they were pointing fingers and laughing at each other.

I was embarrassed to look goofier than I did already. But, once Kimberly came back to our table and put hers on, I felt more comfortable putting mine on too.

Mrs. Cooper demonstrated to us how to soak the bottom of our plexiglass containers with rubbing alcohol.

"But not too wet that it runs off," she warned.

She then instructed us in the safe use of dry ice.

"Dry ice is frozen carbon dioxide. It's much colder than regular ice, about 80 degrees colder. Which means it will burn your skin if you touch it. So, whenever handling the dry ice, be sure to wear the gloves provided."

She went around the room and placed a chunk of dry ice into our plastic storage containers. The ice was smoking. I got the urge to play with it, but I didn't want to get in trouble. Nick had already received a warning.

"Now class," Mrs. Cooper instructed us. "Place the lids on your plexiglass containers, and invert them, place them upside down, over the dry ice. Before I turn out the lights, Kimberly's going to bring each of you a flashlight. Do not turn the flashlights on until I instruct you to."

Kimberly handed me a flashlight, and everyone else in the class.

"Ok, I'm going to turn out the lights now. Give your cloud chambers a few minutes to start working. You'll want to shine your flashlight on the inside of the chamber and make note of what you see."

Mrs. Cooper turned out the lights.

I shined the flashlight on the chamber but didn't see anything, except for a bunch of cloud-like vapors. Mrs. Cooper said that came from the vaporization of the alcohol. The alcohol rises from the base of the container as a gas, but when it sinks toward the dry ice, it becomes a liquid again. I passed the flashlight to Kimberly to see if she could see something.

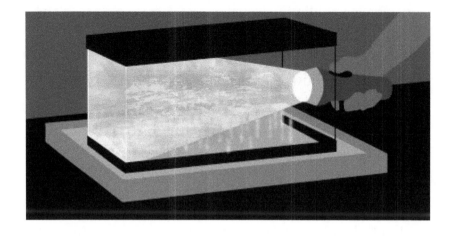

"Oh my!" one student shouted.

"Did you see that?" Sarah said.

"That was SO cool!" Diego said.

"What?" I asked. "What did you see?" We didn't see anything.

I ran over to Sarah's table to see what she was looking at. Sure enough, there were tracks running through her chamber. Things were darting though it. "What is that?" I asked.

"That," Mrs. Cooper responded, "is radiation. You can't see the particles because they're too small."

"Sam, I got it!" Kimberly called over to me. "You gotta see this!"

I ran back to our lab table, and sure enough, there were things making tracks in the vapor.

"What you're seeing," Mrs. Cooper continued, "are the tracks left behind by the radiation. You're seeing alpha particles, beta particles, positrons, and muons. Different particles make different tracks."

"Muons?" I asked.

"Positrons?" Kimberly asked.

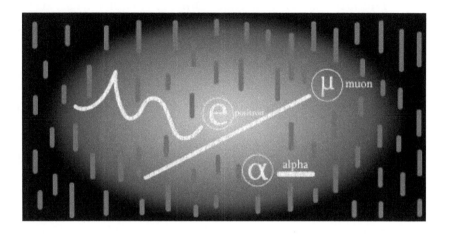

"Muons are negatively charged particles like electrons, but about 200 times as heavy. They come from cosmic radiation. Positrons are positively-charged electrons."

Some particles zipped right through the vapor without stopping. Some particles made curly-cues through the vapor. While others zipped around in straight lines until they bounced off something, like billiard balls.

When Mrs. Cooper turned the lights back on and instructed us on how to put away our chambers, no one wanted to leave. I myself would have gladly missed P.E. Unfortunately, I wasn't given the option.

Mrs. Cooper herself went around collecting the dry ice, while Kimberly and I helped with picking up the plexiglass boxes, plastic containers, alcohol bottles and gloves.

We put our goggles back into the lab drawers just before the bell rang.

The lab was so cool that I almost forgot I was carrying my mom's Geiger counter. I remembered just as we were about to leave.

"You're joining us after school, right?" I said. "We're going to use the Geiger counter to search for the missing uranium."

"Sure," Kimberly said, as she stayed behind to help Mrs. Cooper with something else.

"See you at the lockers," I said, as I left the room, thinking of muons and positrons and alpha particles, and all kinds of cool stuff that I had seen that day.

19

Mr. Phillips, are You Ready for Your Close-Up?

Both Andrea and Kimberly were waiting for me at my locker by the time I made it out of P.E., hair dripping.

"Hey," I said.

"Nice hair," Andrea said, smiling. She knew how self-conscious I was about it.

"Guess what?" Kimberly said.

"What?" Andrea and I responded.

"I got picked for the cheerleading squad!"

"Of course you did," I said.

"You wouldn't have been so sure if you saw my tryout. And I'm up against one other girl for captain of the team."

"You're a shoo-in," Andrea said.

"I wish I were. You should see how good the other girl is. She just moved here from out of state."

"When will you find out?" I asked.

"Ms. Novack's gonna decide after practice on Monday. We're going to do our routine for the President during the assembly. And, the head cheerleader will get to meet him and take a picture with him!"

It was huge news that the President of the United States was coming to Taft Middle School to personally award Mrs. Cooper 'Teacher of Year.' It would be the first time a sitting president had ever come to Willowbrook.

"Lucky," Andrea added.

"In the meantime, we have a rock to find," I said, bringing us back to our quest. Where should we start?"

"Let's get a look at the picture again," Andrea suggested.

I took out my phone and handed it to Andrea so I could retrieve the Geiger counter from my backpack. It was buried under my Geometry book.

"Here it is," I showed them.

"How does it work?" Kimberly asked.

"You just turn it on and bring it next to something you want to test, and it will give off a sound if it's radioactive, just like in Mrs. Cooper's class."

"Cool," said Kimberly.

"I want to try," said Andrea, handing me back my phone.

"Let me use it first. It belongs to the museum, so I can't let anything happen it." I explained.

"What's gonna happen?" Andrea asked.

"Who knows?" I said. "Are you ready?"

"You're gonna turn it on here?" Kimberly asked. Kimberly was still eyeing a few friends, saying her 'goodbyes.' I guess hanging out with geeks could be exacerbated by geeky gadgets like a Geiger counter.

"We don't have to do it here," I said. "We can wait 'til we get to the quad."

The three of us walked over to the quad, anxious to see if the Geiger counter could help us locate the missing uranium.

There were still plenty of kids lingering after the bell, so we thought it was prudent to wait for them to thin out. We sat at our bench on the quad in the meantime.

"I've been thinking more about our project," I said while we were waiting. "I think we need to build the physical model over the weekend, and then I could figure out how to write the code that causes it to give off radioactivity and change into another atom."

Kimberly wasn't paying attention as her boyfriend David Henry was making his way toward us.

"Kim, aren't you coming to Pete's?" he asked.

"Not today David. I told you I had to sort out this missing uranium thing. I can't afford to have it on my record."

"Nothing's going on your record," David assured her. "They can't just blame you for something that you had nothing to do with. They have no proof."

"That may be true. But I don't want anyone even thinking that I had something to do with it."

THE CASE OF THE MISSING URANIUM

"Who cares what others think?" David asked. "All that matters is what I think. And I know you didn't do it."

"I wish it were that easy, David."

Most of the students had left the quad by now. Seeing as I was anxious to get started, and feeling like the third wheel in Kimberly and David's conversation, both Andrea and I got up from the bench and started walking toward the garden area we checked out yesterday. The garden club was evidently not meeting today so we had the area to ourselves. Once we got inside the fenced off area, I turned on the Geiger counter, and before I could bring it near a bunch of rocks I had eyed yesterday, it started going off, making a lot of noises, like it did that morning when I turned it on for a moment.

"Oh my!" Andrea said. "Is that the rock? Is it here?"

"I, uh, don't know," I said.

By then, Kimberly had joined us. If I didn't know better, it looked as if she had been crying.

"That's the sound that Mrs. Cooper's Geiger counter was making in class earlier today! Did you find it?" she asked, hopeful.

"I, uh, every time I turn it on it makes that sound. I'm not sure if it's working right," I said.

"Bring it closer to those rocks over there," Kimberly indicated, wiping a tear from her eye.

I brought the Geiger counter closer, and it continued to make the clicking sound as before. It was hard to tell if the clicking got louder or faster. But it definitely didn't lessen.

"That's it! That's it!" Kimberly shouted.

"I'm not so sure." I said.

"It must be," said Kimberly.

"Well, if it is, we shouldn't get too close. Let's test these other rocks over here," I said.

I led the others to another batch of rocks arranged to beautify the area.

The sporadic clicking continued, but it didn't sound like it got worse when I brought it closer to the rocks. But then again, it didn't lessen either.

In fact, it seemed that everything around us was radioactive, which frightened us to no end.

"How do we know which one is which?" Kimberly asked. "It seems like they're all uranium."

Andrea started singing a new stanza to her song:

Where, oh where has my little rock gone?
Oh where, oh where can it be?
Is it this beep or that, or that beep or this?
Oh where, oh where can it be?

Kimberly was not in the mood. "We're never going to find it. It's everywhere... and it's nowhere."

"We'll find it," I assured Kimberly.

"How can you be so sure?" she asked me.

"We just have to," I said.

"I know," Andrea said. "How about we run the Geiger counter by each locker? If a student took it, and it's still on campus, it's gotta still be in their locker, right?"

"That's a great idea!" Kimberly agreed.

"Ok, but we have to do this systematically. Let's start with the lockers on this side of the school, and proceed from one end to the other," I said.

"Agreed," Kimberly said. She was starting to act like a weight was taken off her shoulders. Surely if it was in school, it's in one of the lockers.

We went back inside and started at one end of the hall. The lockers lined the hall, three rows, both sides. Because we only had one Geiger counter, we had to do this together. We started at the top row and then down to the bottom row, and then back up to the top, and back down, until we covered all the lockers in that hall. We did the same in the opposite direction on the opposite side of the hall. There was nothing besides the usual sporadic clicking. I was growing fearful of the radiation all over the campus. From seeing the reactions of Kimberly and Andrea, they were too.

With no luck in that hall, we moved onto the next hall. We repeated our same methodology. We started at the top row and then moved the counter down to the bottom row, and then back up to the top and so on. The clicking sound was picking up speed the closer we got to the end of the hall, where the principal's office was.

There was no doubt about it. The beeps were getting louder as we edged closer. We had to approach his office quietly, however. If Mr. Phillips knew what we were doing, he'd confiscate the Geiger counter immediately. We might even get detention. Andrea agreed to walk into his front office and speak to his secretary. If the coast were clear, she'd text me.

One of the assistant principals walked out of the office. We turned, facing the lockers, and pretended that Kimberly had just told a hilarious joke.

"Don't you think you girls should be getting along home?" she asked.

"Yes, you're right," I said, pretending that I was having trouble opening the locker door.

"What is that noise?" she asked us, backtracking to where we were standing. Oh my, I forgot to turn off the Geiger counter.

"Oh, uh, nothing." Andrea said. "It's this game of Morse code that we sometimes play after school." I couldn't believe Andrea was able to come up with something so fast.

"I'm a bit of a Morse code aficionado myself," she said, coming in closer to find out more about the game.

"Then you must go," Kimberly said, being so bold that I was sure she was going to get us into trouble. "If we get any help, then we're disqualified, and we really had our hearts set on earning that badge."

"Oh," she said, a little disappointed that she couldn't participate. "But if you need any help, you know where to find me." She walked away, turning back to look at us a couple of more times, as if she were going to say something, and then, thinking better of it, walked off.

"Phew that was close!" Andrea said.

"Quick thinking," I added. "How did you get so devious and diabolical?"

We had a quick chuckle, but we had no time to relish in small victories. Andrea walked into the principal's front office to find Mrs. Pennyweather sitting at her desk. Andrea walked around the room pretending to be looking at the artwork on the walls.

Mrs. Pennyweather, deep into her telephone conversation, didn't look up. Andrea circled Mrs. Pennyweather's desk a few times to see if she could catch a glimpse of whether Mr. Phillips was in his office.

The second time Andrea passed by her desk, Mrs. Pennyweather held her hand over the mouthpiece and asked, "Can I help you?"

"Oh, no thanks," she said. "I was just checking the artwork for an art project I'm doing."

"Well dear, you should be getting home. It's well after school hours."

"Yes, ma'am," Andrea answered. "Just one question, and please don't tell Mr. Phillips cause it's a surprise..."

Just then, Mr. Phillips stepped out of his office, "Madge, a few more things I need to go out in the..."

He stopped when he saw Andrea.

"Andrea, what are you doing here? You should be home by now."

"Yes," Andrea said. "Yes, you're right. I should."

"Andrea was telling me about an art project," Mrs. Pennyweather said.

Andrea looked over at her aghast, after she just told her not to tell Mr. Phillips. "It was supposed to be a surprise, Mrs. Pennyweather," she said.

"My dear, here at Taft we have no surprises," she replied.

"Surprise?" Mr. Phillips's ears perked up. "What surprise?"

"I, uh...," I had to think quickly. "I didn't want to tell you. But I was thinking of drawing a portrait of you for art class. And I was just looking for the perfect spot to hang it."

"You're not taking art this year," said Mr. Phillips suspiciously.

"Yes, you're right." *Think Andrea. Think fast.* "This is, um, for, um an extracurricular project. I was thinking of entering it in the county fair. That's right, the county fair."

"What an excellent idea! Are you going to draw me from a picture, or do you want me to pose for you?"

"Um, I don't know. I hadn't thought that far." I said.

"I think I should pose for you. Let's set up a time in my calendar. Mrs. Pennyweather, will you take care of that?"

"I will," she replied.

He went back in his office, pleased with the idea of his countenance gracing an easel in the country fair.

"When would you like to come in?" she asked.

"Does Mr. Phillips have any time after school tomorrow?"

"Hmm. Tomorrow he has appointments in the afternoon. How about Monday right after school?"

"I have callbacks for Madrigal Singers then."

"Well, let me see," said Mrs. Pennyweather, looking over the calendar. "Tuesday is the President's visit... Hmm... How about Wednesday after school?"

"I can do that," Andrea said.

"Ok, then come here directly after school on Wednesday. Don't be late," Mrs. Pennyweather said. "Mr. Phillips is a very busy man."

"Oh, I know he is. I know he is." And with that, Andrea ran out of the office to tell us what had happened.

We all got quite a laugh imagining Andrea drawing a portrait of Mr. Phillips... for the county fair, of all things. We didn't know which was more ridiculous, Mr. Phillips posing for Andrea, Andrea's lack of artistic ability, or how she could ever place something at the fair. Luckily, it was a long way off until Wednesday.

Seeing as we wouldn't get access to his office today, we decided to go home. All this radioactivity around us was making us nervous anyway.

20

Suit up Girls, We're Going In

My mom was working late tonight so I didn't get a chance to talk to her before bed, and I had so much to talk to her about.

I was glad to find that she was already up by the time I had woken the next morning. I hung out with her in the bathroom while she brushed her teeth.

"What would happen," I asked her, "if we found out a certain place had a lot of radioactivity?"

"Well, I imagine some government agency would be called in, like the Environmental Protection Agency. They'd assess the situation and determine next steps."

"How do they assess it? Do they use a Geiger counter like I used yesterday?"

"I imagine so. I imagine their instrumentation is more sensitive, however. In addition, they can measure the dosage of radiation each individual has been exposed to using a dosimeter."

"Do you have one of those at work?"

"No. We're not regularly exposed to radioactivity at the museum. But anyone who works in a lab in which radiation exposure is likely, usually has a badge that measures the amount of radiation she's exposed to."

"How does someone who works in such a lab keep themselves safe from exposure?" I asked, knowing full well I was asking on behalf of all the students at Taft.

"The badges monitor the proximity and amount of time spent around radioactive materials. So just limiting their exposure is the best line of defense."

"But what if you can't do that? What if you can't avoid it?"

"Those whose work requires them to be exposed to radioactivity I imagine wear special Hazmat suits that are lined with lead to protect vital organs," my mom said, "Like the brain, heart, bone marrow. Why do you ask?"

"Oh, no reason. Just curious," I said, thinking about how I could get my hands on a Hazmat suit in short order.

I went back to my room and texted Andrea and Kimberly.

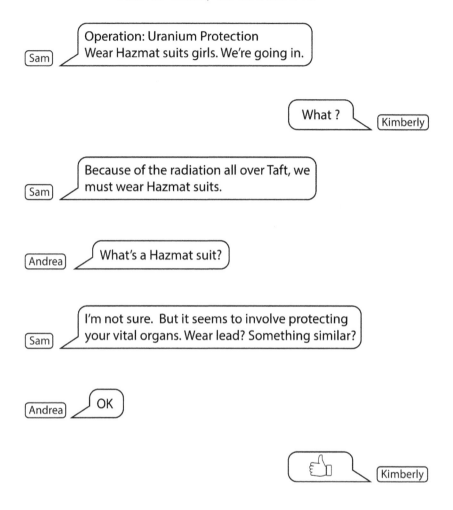

Sam: Operation: Uranium Protection
Wear Hazmat suits girls. We're going in.

Kimberly: What ?

Sam: Because of the radiation all over Taft, we must wear Hazmat suits.

Andrea: What's a Hazmat suit?

Sam: I'm not sure. But it seems to involve protecting your vital organs. Wear lead? Something similar?

Andrea: OK

Kimberly: 👍

Where was I going to find lead in the house? I thought to myself. I didn't know. Still, I grabbed a hat to protect my brain, made sure to wear long pants, socks, and boots. It was a start. And, on the way out of the house, I grabbed a roll of aluminum foil from the kitchen drawer.

"What are gonna do with that?" my dad asked, as he was preparing eggs on the stove.

"It's a school project," I said, which wasn't completely untrue. "I'm also looking for a cookie sheet," I said, opening and closing cupboards to find them.

My dad reached into a cupboard next to the oven and pulled one out. "Will this do?" he asked.

"Yeah, but I need two."

"Two?" he asked, pulling out an additional one.

"Are you baking cookies?" he asked.

"Nope," I said.

I ran upstairs with my cookie sheets and foil. I used my wire cutters to poke holes into the cookie sheets, and ran wires through them to hang like a sandwich board in front and behind me.

I grabbed my stuff and ran downstairs to meet Andrea on the way to school. "I'll see you later," I said on my way out the door.

"Aren't you going to have breakfast?" he asked.

"No time today Dad. I love you."

"I, uh, love you..." his voice trailed off as I shut the door behind me and hurried to our meeting point.

21

If Looks Could Kill

Andrea texted me that she was running late putting her Hazmat suit together and that I shouldn't wait for her.

By the time I arrived at school, I had finished assembling my suit. I was wearing the cookie sheet sandwich board, and had covered my hat, both inside and out, with aluminum foil. My vital organs were well-protected. Kimberly showed up minutes later, wearing knight armor for a top. Her pants were awfully bulky, and it seemed as if she couldn't bend her knees. She confided in me that she was wearing three pairs of pants.

"Where did you get the knight suit?" I asked her.

"Funny thing. My parents had inherited it from my grandparents. We used to play with it in the attic. But I had no idea how to get the leggings on."

"Wow, you're really protected," I commented.

"I don't know. This thing is so heavy that I can hardly move."

Just then Andrea appeared covered in pie pans and foil. We could hear the snickering from the other kids around us.

"I don't think I thought this through," Kimberly said. "I wish people would stop staring."

"At least we're safe!" I said to those within ear shot. "If you knew what was happening on campus, you'd protect yourselves too!"

David Henry came by to take Kimberly to first period.

"What are you wearing?" he asked her in disbelief.

"There's radiation all over the place. I'm trying to keep myself safe." Kimberly said.

David was speechless.

"I, uh, forgot I have to see my counselor about something before the bell rings," he said, trying to make a quick getaway.

"But the bell's going to ring any minute," Kimberly protested.

With that, David distanced himself even more from Kimberly and hurried down the hall.

Kimberly looked back at us, with what looked like tears welling in her eyes.

"Maybe he really did have to see his counselor," Andrea consoled her.

"I can't go around wearing this in public," she said. "I. Just. Can't."

I took the Geiger counter out from my backpack and turned it on to remind her how dangerous our school was.

The random, scattered clicking noises helped prioritize her worries.

"Still, I think I'd rather light up like a Christmas tree from all the radiation than be the school's pariah."

"Well, I don't think you'll have to make that choice," I assured her. "We're going to get to the bottom of this, return the uranium, and they'll be calling us heroes when we make the school safe again."

"Are you sure?" Kimberly asked.

"Of course I'm sure."

The bell rang. Kimberly faked a smile and the three of us went our separate ways. The truth was, I wasn't sure. But I wasn't nearly as concerned what other people thought of me. After all, I already felt like an outcast. Kimberly, on the other hand, had much further to fall.

22

Half-Lives!

By the time we got to fifth period, I had ditched the sandwich board, and I was holding my aluminum foil hat in my hand. Kimberly was no longer wearing her knight armor. It looked as if she had cried more than once that day. Clearly, I did not think through our Operation: Uranium Protection well enough. It was humiliating being pointed at, laughed at, and called the "tin man." I can just imagine what Kimberly went through.

"Are you ok?" I asked Kimberly, but before she had the chance to respond, Mrs. Cooper had quieted us down and asked for our attention.

She reminded us that all the protons, the positively-charged particles in an atom, were contained in the nucleus. And that these protons can leak out of the nuclei in the form of alpha particles, beta particles, and positrons, changing an atom's core identity.

She called this change in the identity of an atom transmutation.

Boy, I'd like to have transmuted to anyone else after today. Human beings, however, don't seem to have this option.

Mrs. Cooper also reviewed shielding, a concept that both Kimberly and I had learned first-hand. "Remember to keep a distance from a radioactive source and limit the time you are exposed."

Kimberly and I looked at each other and started laughing. We just couldn't help ourselves.

"Ladies," Mrs. Cooper singled us out. "Would you mind sharing with the rest of the class what you find so funny about this?"

"I wouldn't know where to start," I said, rather boldly for even me.

"Well, straighten yourselves out and let me continue," she said.

"It's just that," Kimberly, emboldened, said, "there's radiation all over the school. We're here all day long and we can't possibly maintain our distance or time of exposure."

This revelation caused commotion throughout the class.

"What do you mean?" Mrs. Cooper asked.

"My mom lent me this Geiger counter," I said, pulling the counter out of my backpack, "and it tells me there's radiation all over school."

I turned it on so that she could hear the clicking too.

The rest of the class was looking back and forth between the Geiger counter and Mrs. Cooper, eager to get her reaction.

"You can turn that off now, Sam," Mrs. Cooper said.

"Remember there's naturally occurring radioactivity all around us," she continued. "We watched cosmic rays in the atmosphere give off alpha particles, beta particles and muons in our cloud chambers yesterday. You cannot avoid all radiation. In fact, these cosmic rays are the result of the Big Bang 13.7 billion years ago. Not only are you exposed to them on an ongoing basis, but so were your parents, grandparents, and great grandparents. Our bodies are equipped to deal with small amounts of radiation. What you're seeing around school is just that, small unavoidable doses."

"So we don't have to be concerned?" I asked.

"No," Mrs. Cooper said, smiling, "no one needs be concerned."

Both Kimberly and I looked at each other and started laughing again.

"Ok, now that we've assuaged everybody's fears, let's move onto today's topic - half-lives. Some radioactive atoms give off particles faster than others. When an atom's nucleus gives off particles, it's called radioactive decay."

She wrote "Radioactive Decay" on the white board.

RADIOACTIVE DECAY

"The rate of decay is called a half-life. Which is exactly what it sounds like. The time it takes for half of a sample of atoms to decay."

Mrs. Cooper wrote "Half-Life" underneath "Radioactive Decay."

RADIOACTIVE DECAY
HALF-LIFE

As she was presenting the lesson, I quietly put away the remnants of my Hazmat suit that would fit in my backpack and balled up the foil to throw away.

"So, if you have 8 radioactive atoms with a half-life of 1 day, that means that over the course of one day, half of the atoms will decay, leaving four remaining.

$$8 \xrightarrow{\text{1 day}} 4$$
$$\text{remaining} \quad \text{remaining}$$

At the end of day 2, half of those four unchanged atoms would decay as well, leaving just two behind unchanged.

$$8 \xrightarrow{\text{1 day}} 4 \xrightarrow{\text{1 day}} 2$$

remaining   remaining   remaining

At the end of day 3, one of the remaining two will have decayed as well.

$$8 \xrightarrow{\text{1 day}} 4 \xrightarrow{\text{1 day}} 2 \xrightarrow{\text{1 day}} 1$$

remaining   remaining   remaining

Some atoms have much longer half-lives, like potassium-40. Its half-life is 1.3 billion years.

Carbon-14, which is used to date fossils, has a half-life of 5,730 years.

Radium-222, on the other hand, has a half-life of only 38 seconds."

I just had a thought that I needed to tell Kimberly. As I wasn't going to interrupt Mrs. Cooper again, I took out my notebook and wrote the following:

> Half-lives? Could the uranium
> have lost half its mass because
> half of it decayed?

Kimberly drew a happy face right below my suggestion.

I was so excited by this that I could hardly contain myself. Of course! Half-lives! Half of it decayed! But why didn't Mrs. Cooper think of that in the first place, I thought to myself. After all, it was so obvious.

"Kimberly and I are going to hand out a bag of M&Ms to each table. Do not open them. And especially, do not eat them. After you perform the experiment according to the instructions I give you, then you will be able to eat them, but not now."

Kimberly gave each table a bag of M&Ms and a paper cup while Mrs. Cooper described the activity.

"You're first going to put your results in a table like this.

#HALF - LIVES	#M+MS REMAINING
0	40

"Next, empty your bags and count the number of M&Ms you're starting with."

"Then, place all the M&Ms into your paper cup, shake them around, and empty them gently on the table.

"All the M&Ms that land face down are considered 'decayed.' You're going to remove them from the pile and count only the remaining face-up M&Ms.

"These are the number of Mm isotopes remaining after the first half-life. Record this number in your table.

"You will scoop these up, return them to the cup and do the whole thing over again until you have no more Mm isotope remaining.

"After you complete your table, you will plot your results as a decay graph of the Mm isotope. Place the number of half-lives on the X-axis at the bottom of the graph, and the number of Mms remaining on the y-axis, like this:

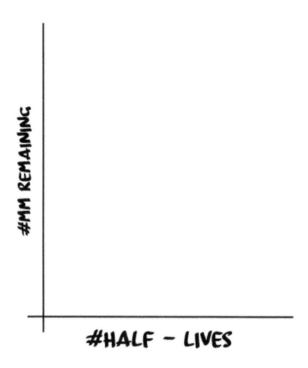

"Once you finish plotting, draw a smooth curve through the points and describe the shape of the graph. Only once you've completed the graph and shown it to me, you are allowed to eat your M&Ms.

"Any questions? No? Then begin."

The class immediately broke into loud chatter as students opened their M&M bags, poured out the candies and counted them.

I opened our bag, poured it on the table, and the two of us counted them, me in pairs and Kimberly singly.

"44," I said.

"That's what I got too," Kimberly agreed.

I scooped up the M&Ms and placed them in the paper cup. I covered the top with my hand, gave it a few good shakes, and then poured them on the table. We both removed the M&Ms that landed face down and then counted the remaining ones. We counted, "21."

#HALF - LIVES	#M+MS REMAINING
0	44
1	21

I scooped up the remaining M&Ms, put them back in the cup, and handed the cup over to Kimberly.

She shook and poured them back on the table. We again removed the M&Ms that landed face-down, and counted the remaining M&Ms.

"12."

#HALF - LIVES	#M+MS REMAINING
0	44
1	21
2	12

Kimberly scooped up the remaining M&Ms, put them back in the cup, shook and poured them back on the table. Again, we removed the M&Ms that landed face-down and counted the remaining ones.

"5."

#HALF - LIVES	#M+MS REMAINING
0	44
1	21
2	12
3	5

We took turns with the cup and our remaining values were 3, 2, 1, 1, 1, 0.

#HALF – LIVES	#M+MS REMAINING
0	44
1	21
2	12
3	5
4	3
5	2
6	1
7	1
8	1
9	0

Our plot looked like this.

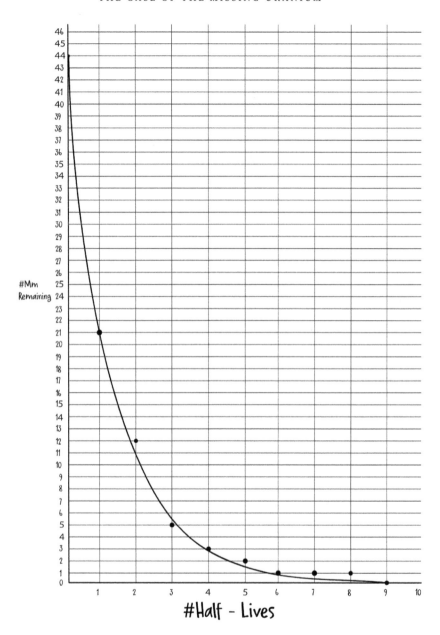

Mrs. Cooper walked over to our table to check our graph, approved it, and gave us permission to eat the M&Ms. But we had something else to discuss with her.

"Mrs. Cooper," I said. "Wouldn't half of the uranium atoms decay in its first half-life?"

"Yes," she said.

"So isn't it obvious that Kimberly had nothing to do with the missing uranium? That it decayed on its own, naturally?"

"Excellent question, Sam. Let me respond in two ways. First, when uranium decays by giving off an alpha particle, its mass only decreases by four — two protons and two neutrons. First, figure out how many decay sequences would have to happen for U-238 to get down to half its mass. Let me know when you figure out that number."

"We will," I said, and tore out a piece of lined paper from my notebook.

I wrote at the top of the paper 238 —> 234.

$$1.\ 238 \longrightarrow 234$$

Half of 238 is 119, so I needed to figure out how many half-lives would have to pass to get down to 119.

1. 238 —> 234
2. 234 —> 230
3. 230 —> 226
4. 226 —> 222
5. 222 —> 218
6. 218 —> 214
7. 214 —> 210
8. 210 —> 206
9. 206 —> 202
10. 202 —> 198
11. 198 —> 194
12. 194 —> 190
13. 190 —> 186
14. 186 —> 182
15. 182 —> 178
16. 178 —> 174
17. 174 —> 170
18. 170 —> 166
19. 166 —> 162
20. 162 —> 158
21. 158 —> 154
22. 154 —> 150
23. 150 —> 146
24. 144 —> 140
25. 140 —> 136
26. 136 —> 132
27. 132 —> 128
28. 128 —> 124
29. 124 —> 120
30. 120 —> 116

It would take between 29 and 30 half-lives to get to 119.

Kimberly raised her hand to get Mrs. Cooper's attention.

Mrs. Cooper came over quickly, as most of the rest of the class was busy eating M&Ms.

I showed her how we had figured that it would take between 29 and 30 half-lives for uranium-238 to lose half its mass.

"Good work," Mrs. Cooper commended us. "Now, go research how long each half-life of uranium-238 is. Then we'll talk."

As she walked away, Kimberly and I knew what we needed to do. We decided to meet in the library after school to research the half-life of uranium-238.

We split our M&Ms between us, cleaned up, and parted ways when the bell rang.

23

Do Rocks Read Personals Ads?

Kimberly was already looking up uranium's half-life in what seemed to be the biggest book in the world. As she was looking, I lifted the cover off the table to read its title: "CRC Handbook of Chemistry and Physics."

"Where'd you get that?" I asked.

"Mrs. Ferguson suggested I use it." Mrs. Ferguson was the school librarian. She always knew how to find exactly what we were looking for. There were other tables occupied by students talking among themselves while Mrs. Ferguson walked among them reminding them to be quiet.

"Did you know there are 25 isotopes of uranium in all?" Kimberly asked, as she was looking for our answer.

"I did not know that. I imagine they all have the same half-life, no?"

"That's what I thought too, but each of the 25 isotopes has its own half-life. Which one are we looking for again?"

"Uranium-238," I reminded her.

"Uranium-238," Kimberly repeated over and over to herself as she skimmed the page with her index finger from top to bottom.

"What are you guys doing here?" asked Andrea as she joined us at the table. She too had lost most of her Hazmat suit over the course of the day.

"We're looking for the half-life of uranium." I said."

"Uranium-238," said Kimberly as her finger stopped on that particular isotope.

"Half-life? Is that like something that's half alive, and half dead? Like zombies?"

Andrea and I laughed.

"No," I said. "It's the amount of time it takes for half of an atom sample to decay into another atom.

"4.5 billion years," Kimberly read out loud.

"4.5 billion?" I asked Kimberly, making sure I heard her correctly.

"Let me see that." I got up and looked at what her finger was pointing to. She was right. The half-life of uranium-238 was 4.5 billion years.

"What does that mean?" Andrea asked.

"It means that there's no way that half of the uranium sample in Mrs. Cooper's room could have decayed to half its size in the past week, month, or even year!" It would take 4.5 billion years for just one half-life, and we'd need like 29 of them. That's 29 times 4.5 billion years!"

"So we're back to where we started," Kimberly said.

"Not exactly," I said. "We did find out that there's cosmic radiation all around us. And, that it's s natural part of the universe."

"And we did find out that the half-life of uranium-238 is 4.5 billion years," Kimberly added.

"Which tells us that uranium's half-life couldn't be responsible for losing half its mass," I added.

"And," Andrea added, "We did schedule an appointment with Mr. Phillips to paint his portrait!"

"The portrait! I forgot all about that!" I said.

Mrs. Ferguson looked over at us with the look that means we were making too much noise.

We went back to whispering.

"Yeah, and while I'm busy making a fool out of myself pretending to draw," Andrea said, "you can sneak around his office for the source of the radiation!"

"Yes, that's right!" I said. "Remember Kimberly, it did seem to get stronger as we got closer to his office."

"Do you really think the principal stole the missing uranium?" Kimberly asked in disbelief.

"I don't know what to believe anymore. Do you have any other ideas?" I asked.

"I have one," Kimberly said.

"Go on, we're listening," Andrea added.

"What if we set a trap for the thief?" Kimberly said.

"What kind of trap?" I asked.

"What if we got the word out that there was more uranium to be had, and catch the person in the act?" Kimberly asked.

"How would we do that?" I asked.

"I know," Andrea said. "We could put an ad in Monday morning's bulletin."

"What kind of ad? Uranium for sale? I doubt the administration would sign off on that," I said. "Besides, how do we ensure that the person who claims the rock is the same person who stole the other half?"

"It'd have to be in the way we write the ad."

Mrs. Ferguson came to our table to remind us that we were too loud.

"This is a library after all," she said.

We apologized and proceeded to quietly wordsmith the following ad:

What's better than half a rock?
The other half, of course!
Come to the quad benches after school to claim.

I folded up the ad, and the three of us walked it over to the school newspaper office, which was already locked. I added a note to the back of it saying:

URGENT: For Monday's
announcements.

And dropped it through the slit in the door.

24

Men in Black

Just as we dropped off the ad, we saw three men in black suits and dark sunglasses walk into the principal's office.

We looked at each other, trying to make sense of what we just saw.

"You did say that as we walked closer to Mr. Phillips's office the amount of radiation increased," Kimberly reminded us.

"Yes, and remember, I stumbled upon a private meeting between Mr. Phillips and Mrs. Cooper, and they were clearly discussing the uranium," I said. "And he made it perfectly clear that he didn't want me involved. In fact, his exact words were, 'You shouldn't be putting your nose into school business.' Or did he mean, his business?"

"Then it must be him!" said Andrea. "And to think, I was going to paint his portrait!"

"His stick-figure portrait!" I added. "Well, let's walk into Mrs. Pennyweather's office to see what we can snoop out."

The three of us meandered into Mrs. Pennyweather's office, trying to look inconspicuous. We said hi to Mrs. Pennyweather and then proceeded to look around at the artwork on the walls.

"May I help you ladies?" she asked us.

I walked over to her and asked, "Is Mr. Phillips available?"

"Mr. Phillips is in a very important meeting," she said. "What is this in regard to?"

"Oh, it's well, secret business."

"Secret business?" Mrs. Pennyweather asked.

"You know, the kind of secret business that 13 year old girls get themselves into," I said.

"Oh," Mrs. Pennyweather said, appearing to know what I was talking about, but really having no clue.

"Well, he won't be available the rest of today," she said. "Perhaps you can try again on Monday."

"Hmm. Yes. I suppose you're right." I was trying to read who he was meeting with, from his calendar which was laying open on Mrs. Pennyweather's desk. It was difficult to read, being upside-down and all.

"Yes," I said. "I can try again on Monday. Come on girls," I said to Andrea and Kimberly. We started to walk outside of the office.

"One more thing," I said, turning back to Mrs. Pennyweather. "Mr. Phillips told me earlier today that he'd be available after school. Do you know why his plans changed?"

"There are certain things even the principal can't say no to," she said.

With that, the three of us left the office.

"Wow, you were great," Andrea said to me.

"I didn't get any new information though. I have no idea who those men in black are, but I'm certain they have something to do with the missing uranium."

"Yes, me too," agreed Kimberly. "Why else would they be having a secret meeting with Mr. Phillips? They certainly don't look like parents."

"Do you suppose we should..." I began to say, when the principal, accompanied by the three men in black, walked out of Mrs. Pennyweather's office.

"Young ladies, how many times have I told you to go home. You shouldn't be lingering around here after school unless you are being supervised by an adult. This is my last warning!" he said.

"Yes Mr. Phillips," the three of us said in unison.

We turned to walk away, so that he'd think we were leaving. But we weren't about to leave. Not just yet.

Instead, we huddled together.

25

Caught Red-Handed

"This is our chance!" I whispered. "One of you needs to follow them to see where they go. And one of you needs to distract Mrs. Pennyweather so I can go search for the missing uranium in Mr. Phillips's office."

"I'll follow them," Kimberly volunteered.

"Great," I said. "That means Andrea, you come with me."

Kimberly followed the four men.

Andrea and I returned to Mrs. Pennyweather's office.

"We're back," I said to Mrs. Pennyweather. "Are you sure Mr. Phillips can't talk right now?"

"Yes I'm sure," Mrs. Pennyweather said. "But if you leave me a note, I'll make sure to give it to him."

"Well, the thing is," I moved in closer to her, "It's not really my problem, you know what I'm saying? It's really, well," I looked over to Andrea, "It's really Andrea's problem. And I agreed to come with her and help her talk to him."

"Uh huh," Mrs. Pennyweather said.

"Andrea," I said, calling Andrea over.

"Do you mind?" I said to Mrs. Pennyweather, getting her permission after the fact.

"Andrea, will you come here?" I asked.

Andrea approached Mrs. Pennyweather's desk.

"Andrea, Mrs. Pennyweather says that Mr. Phillips won't be available the rest of the day, but you can leave him a note."

Andrea started crying on cue. She was masterful. Through her tears, she started telling Mrs. Pennyweather her story.

"It's about my mom. She has a twin sister in El Salvador who she hasn't seen in 13 years. May I sit down?" she asked, as she sat in the chair opposite.

"There, there," Mrs. Pennyweather said. She scooted her box of tissues toward Andrea. Andrea grabbed one. Then two. Then three.

"And her letters aren't being returned anymore," she continued. "And she's afraid... she's afraid... that something bad has happened to her.

"You see it all started when she went to work at the local coffee bean factory. She was working long hours and not making enough money. In fact, my mother would send her money every month to make ends meet. She has five children to feed. And when she'd work those long hours..."

Once I saw that Mrs. Pennyweather was fully engrossed in Andrea's made-up story, I ducked into Mr. Phillips's office to take a look around. I decided not to use the Geiger counter in my backpack, afraid that its beeping would alert Mrs. Pennyweather. Armed only with the picture of the pitchblende on my phone, I snooped into Mr. Phillips's desk drawers and bookshelves. I looked under and behind knick-knacks, inside his potted plants, feeling in the soil for anything buried from prying eyes. And I looked through the drawers of his file cabinet.

I was in the second drawer from the top when the door opened, and in came both Mr. Phillips and Mrs. Pennyweather.

"Ms. Gold, what do you think you're doing?" Mr. Phillips asked.

"Oh, I, uh, I thought I had left a school paper in here. Am I not supposed to be looking in here?" I asked, trying to seem all innocent.

Behind Mr. Phillips and Mrs. Pennyweather were Andrea and Kimberly.

"I caught your two friends snooping around too. This is breaking and entering. I have half a mind to call the police on you. But I won't. But rest assured I will be bringing your parents in on this. The three of you girls are looking at detention every day next week. And you can forget about attending Tuesday's assembly and meeting the President. We'll make alternate arrangements."

"Not Monday!" Andrea said, pleading. "I have my call back on Monday!"

"And I have cheerleading practice!"

And I so wanted to meet the President. In my whole life, I had never met a president. And, we had a uranium thief to catch, who we had set out a trap for (though I chose not to divulge that information).

"Well, you girls should have thought about that before you broke the rules, eh?" Mr. Phillips said. "Now wait in Mrs. Pennyweather's office as I call your parents to pick you up."

My mom was going to be super angry with me. She did not like being taken away from the museum in the middle of the afternoon to begin with. And being caught red-handed in the principal's office — I imagined I'd be grounded for life. It seemed from their facial expressions that Andrea and Kimberly were equally worried.

The three of us walked back out into Mrs. Pennyweather's office and waited to be picked up.

We didn't talk for the longest time, contemplating how we were going to explain ourselves to our parents.

Finally, I whispered to Kimberly, "Well, what did you find out about the men in black?"

"Mr. Phillips walked them out to a black car that was waiting for them. When one of them reached into his pocket, I thought I saw something like the glint of a gun. I was too far away to get a close enough look. It was then that one of them made eye contact with me causing Mr. Phillips to spin around and see me too. I was about to run away when he told me to freeze exactly where I was. I didn't know what to do. So I froze."

"Yeah," Andrea said, "And when Mr. Phillips entered the office with Kimberly, I could tell that the gig was up.

"'Oh, Mr. Phillips, I've been waiting to talk to you!'," I said, keeping in character. But he knew something was fishy. And once he saw you rummaging through his office, we were all toast."

"And now I'm going to miss callbacks. I'll never get into the Madrigal Singers now," Andrea said.

"And I'll never get to be cheerleading captain now," Kimberly said.

"And it's all my fault," I said.

"How is it your fault?" Kimberly asked.

"Well, this whole scheme was my idea."

"No, it was our idea," Andrea said.

"Yeah, and you two were only doing it to help me prove my innocence," Kimberly added. "And now, look where we are. I think my parents would rather have a daughter who was a uranium thief, than a daughter who was caught up in an international smuggling ring."

"I'm beginning to think it would have been a whole lot easier if we had just stuck to our original project idea — making a model of the atom out of styrofoam balls."

Andrea and Kimberly started laughing. Mrs. Pennyweather looked up as if to remind us how much trouble we were in. We didn't need reminding.

My dad was the last of the three parents to show up. By the time he arrived, the other two had left. To be honest, I would have rather it been my mom. I think in some small way she might have understood. My dad would not. When he came in, he was immediately called into the principal's office, and then I was summoned in as well. The look my father gave me spoke volumes. He was clearly deeply disappointed in me.

"I assure you Mr. Phillips that this is the last time you will ever need to bring Sam into your office. We have clearly given her more leeway than her maturity allows. What do you have to say for yourself, Samantha Leah?" my father asked.

I knew I was in serious trouble when he called me by my full name.

We didn't talk the entire ride home. I would have preferred that he said something - anything. The silence was killing me. I decided to break it.

"I'm sorry Dad," I said.

"What in the world were you thinking Samantha?" he responded.

I started to explain, but he interrupted me. "I don't want to hear it. In fact, as soon as we get home, you're grounded indefinitely."

"Indefinitely?" I asked.

"Indefinitely," he responded.

"What are you going to say to Mom?" I asked.

"I'm going to tell her exactly what Mr. Phillips told me."

That's what I was afraid of.

26

What are Little Brothers for?

Having spent most of the weekend in my room, I was not only getting stir crazy, but anxious about school tomorrow. Kimberly and I had barely started on our science project. She was of course grounded too. As was Andrea. Kimberly did text me however that she had convinced her mom to drive her to the store to buy some styrofoam balls and paint to make the atomic model. I busied myself with figuring out how to code the LED lights on my Raspberry Pi to change from green to red —after the first alpha particle was given off — to blue — when a beta particle was given off.

Uranium-238 has 92 protons. When it loses an alpha particle, it loses 2 protons and becomes Thorium-234. Thorium-234 has 90 protons. When Thorium-234 gives off a beta particle, it gains one proton back, becoming Protactinium-234. Protactinium-234 has 91 protons.

$$^{238}_{92}\text{U} \rightarrow {}^{234}_{90}\text{Th}{+}\ {}^{4}_{2}\text{He} \rightarrow {}^{234}_{91}\text{Pa}{+}\ {}^{0}_{-1}\text{e}$$

green   red   alpha particle   blue

To be honest, though, my heart wasn't in it. I felt terrible for letting my parents down. And I let Kimberly down because I hadn't found the missing uranium. We were so close, too. Too close. If Mr. Phillips were indeed the uranium smuggler, how could we prove it? We couldn't risk sneaking around his office again. And then, we had set up a trap for the smuggler tomorrow after school. But we wouldn't be there, because all three of us were given detention.

My phone signaled a text had come through. It was from Kimberly.

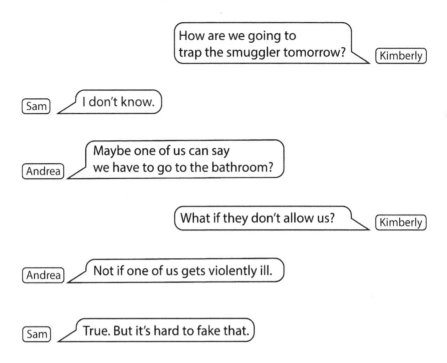

Just then, Alex swung my door open and snapped my picture. I was a mess. I was still in my pajamas.

"Alex!" I yelled. "Mom! Alex is doing it again!"

"This picture will be perfect for the yearbook," Alex said. "Sam Gold - grounded."

"You wouldn't dare."

"Oh, but I would," Alex said.

I got up and slammed the door on him and went back to the texts.

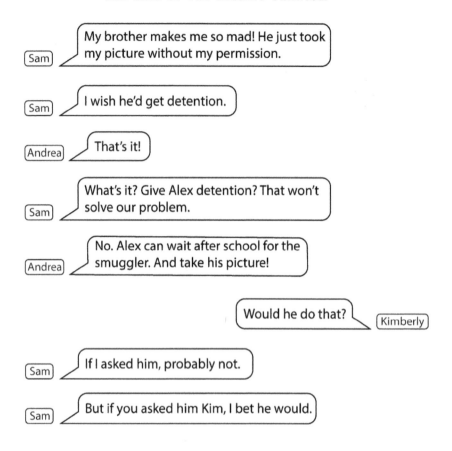

Alex had had a crush on Kimberly ever since elementary school. He was like a puppy dog in her presence, always following her around.

The last thing I wanted to do was to be beholden to my little brother. It placed me in an uncomfortable position. But it seemed to be the only viable idea.

"Alex!" I called out, opening the door.

There was no answer.

"Alex, I need to talk to you," I said.

"I don't care what you say. This picture's going in the yearbook," Alex responded from his bedroom.

"That's fine. Keep the picture. I just need to talk to you." There was no answer.

"Please," I said, all nice and sweet, almost gagging over it.

"Yeah, what?" he answered, popping his head out of his bedroom door.

"I need a favor."

"No way."

"I haven't even told you what the favor is," I said.

"The answer's still no."

"You know, the favor's not for me anyway, it's for Kimberly."

His eyes perked up.

"Yes, Kimberly needs a favor," I said.

"Then why doesn't she ask me herself," Alex said.

"She will," I said. "I'll get her on the phone for you if you come here."

"How do I know this isn't a trap?" he asked.

"I'll call her right now." I rang her on my cell phone and put it on speaker.

"Kimberly?"

"Yes," she replied.

"My brother wants to speak to you."

I held the phone out to Alex, who came out into the hallway to answer it.

"Hi?" Alex said.

"Hi Alex. I need your help," Kimberly's voice sounded through the speaker phone.

"What kind of help?"

"I need you to take some pictures in the quad after school tomorrow."

"What kind of pictures?"

Kimberly explained what we needed him to do. Alex of course agreed. After all, as I said before, he'd do anything for Kimberly.

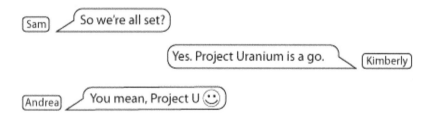

We signed off for the evening. Kimberly would finish making the atom model, and when I got to school, I'd insert the Raspberry Pi into it.

27

Detention, Ugh!

I heard our announcement read over the loudspeaker during homeroom:

> *What's better than half a rock?*
> *The other half, of course!*
> *Come to the quad benches after school to claim.*

Our Raspberry Pi atom went off flawlessly. Mrs. Cooper loved it and wanted to keep it to show her students next year. I sort of wanted my Raspberry Pi back, but I wasn't going to say no to her. At least, not now.

Two hours later we met up in detention. We weren't allowed to talk to each other. For the entire hour, we had to work silently. I however couldn't possibly get any work done. I took out my math textbook to look as if I were reading it, but I could only think about the quad, the thief, and my undependable brother Alex. What if the thief didn't show? What if Alex forgot? What if he didn't take a picture? All these what-ifs were running loops through my head.

Kimberly passed me a note by way of the student in-between us. I made sure to take it when the teacher wasn't looking. I opened the note.

Operation Uranium should have decayed by now.

I looked over at Kimberly, nodded in agreement, and proceeded to write a note back to her.

I sure hope Ansel Adams comes through.

Ansel Adams was a famous landscape photographer in the 1900s. I figured Kimberly would get the reference.

After I put the final period on the sentence, I doodled a picture of Alex with his tongue sticking out.

I put the final period on the note, folded it up, when a hand appeared on my desk asking for the note. My heart skipped a beat. The hand belonged to Coach Billingsley, the teacher in charge of detention.

I looked up at him sheepishly.

"You know you're not allowed to be passing notes during detention Ms. Gold. Hand it over," he said.

I could hear my heart pounding in my ears. I wanted to look over to Kimberly and Andrea, but I didn't want to rat them out. Catching me in the act was one thing. Bringing along my two friends was another.

"It's, uh, nothing," I told him.

"Hand it over," he insisted.

"I, uh." The truth was, there was nothing I could say or do, other than hand over the note. Which is what I did.

Coach Billingsley took the note back with him to the front of the class, opened it, and read it aloud to the class.

Operation Uranium should have

decayed by now. I sure hope

Ansel Adams comes through.

I turned beet red as I sank into my seat. The other students laughed.

"And here is an original by the talented up-and-coming young artist Sam Gold," he said, showing the class the picture. Hopefully, it was too small for anyone to really get a glimpse of.

I was mortified.

"Ms. Gold, apparently you think that you can disrespect the rules of detention. Well, that kind of behavior has earned you another detention, should we say tomorrow, same time, same place?"

I could feel everyone's eyes were on me, but I didn't want to make eye contact with any one of them. I looked down at my desk.

"Uh, I, already have detention tomorrow," I said. A week of detention wasn't nearly as bad as being called out in front of everyone in the whole school, or what seemed like everyone -- this was unbearable.

"Then we'll tack another detention onto that."

I stared directly at the back of the student's desk in front of me for the rest of the hour. It felt like the hour would never end. When we were dismissed, I wanted to explain myself to Coach Billingsley, but I couldn't at the time. We had a smuggler to catch.

I couldn't get out of the room soon enough, so it wasn't a surprise that I was the first one out the door. I ran straight to my locker, not waiting for Andrea or Kimberly. They showed up seconds later.

28

The One in Which All Answers are Revealed

"Oh wow," Andrea said. "Just wow."

"I know," I said. "I don't think I've been more embarrassed in my life!" I said.

"Thank you for not turning me in," Kimberly said.

"I'd never do that," I said.

"I wanted to punch him in the nose!" Andrea said.

I looked at her quizzically.

"Just sayin'," she added.

"It's just a detention," I said, trying to dismiss the event as best I could. "Where's Alex? He should be here by now."

We were foolish to base our plan on my little brother Alex. He was not someone I could count on. In fact, he was just the opposite. How many times did he go out of his way to mess with me? How could I have been so foolish as to pin our plan on him?

Just then, I was relieved to see Alex walking toward us, talking with Earl the custodian.

"Hi Earl," I said.

"Hi girls," he responded. "It's getting late, shouldn't you be home by now?"

"We had detention," I said.

"Detention?" Earl asked. "I won't ask you what for. Just hurry it up and get home so you can come back ready to learn tomorrow. Never put your education on the back burner, detention or not."

"We will," I said, glad that he was walking away so we could get the scoop from Alex.

"Well, what happened?" I blurted out. "Did he show up?"

"Let me show you my pictures!" Alex said, eager to impress Kimberly.

He opened his camera roll and showed us the picture of the bench we had established as the rendezvous point. He swiped that picture to the right and showed us another picture of the empty bench."

"Look at this one," he said, showing us a third picture of an empty bench. "Notice how the vivid warm filter brings out the browns and oranges.

"Now, I applied a monochrome picture filter to this one," swiping left to reveal another picture. "It looks like one of our parents' old black and whites.

"And this one," he said, swiping left again, "I added sepia tones."

"These are all pictures of an empty bench!" I said. "Did anyone show???" I demanded, running out of patience.

"Hold your horses," he said to me, eager to show Kimberly more pictures from his camera roll.

"Here's one with the rainbow filter," he showed Kimberly.

"And this one," he said, swiping left again, I put a dog nose and ears on Earl."

"Earl? Did anyone show up other than Earl?" I asked.

"No, just Earl," Alex replied, still showing pictures to Kimberly. Andrea was looking on. I had lost my patience.

I knew that leaving such a critical job to Alex was a huge mistake.

Operation Uranium was a failure. We would never find the missing uranium. I had let Kimberly down. And, I had roped Andrea into the consequences of my life of crime.

Just then, I saw the men in black coming toward us, popping in and out of classrooms as they did.

Earl came back over to us to tell us we really needed to leave.

"The Secret Service is closing down the school," he said.

"Secret Service?" I asked.

"Yeah, for the President's visit tomorrow. They need to seal the perimeter ahead of time," Earl said.

"Those men in black are the secret service?" I asked him incredulously. "You mean, they're not part of an international uranium smuggling operation?"

"What?" Earl asked, chuckling. "It sounds like you've been reading too many spy novels."

"So maybe the principal didn't take it," I said to Kimberly and Andrea. "And maybe he doesn't have connections with an international smuggling operation. And maybe he was just preparing for the President's visit," I said.

"Ok now, it's time to go home," Earl repeated.

"And therefore no one showed up to the rendezvous because there was no smuggling ring in the first place," Andrea added, as if she didn't hear Earl.

"No one but Earl," I added.

"Yeah, but it still doesn't account for the missing uranium," said Kimberly.

No one but Earl. The words had come out of my mouth before I had really considered them. *No one but Earl.*

"Missing uranium? What are you girls talking about?" Earl asked.

Could Earl have taken the uranium rock? After all, he did have access to every room on campus.

"Earl," I began. "Do you know anything about a piece of uranium that went missing from Mrs. Cooper's storeroom?"

"Uranium? From Mrs. Cooper's storeroom? You know that Mrs. Cooper couldn't possibly have any uranium on campus. You kids and your fanciful stories. If there was any uranium in this school, OSHA would be on us like a fly to honey. C'mon kids, you best get home."

"No, I'm serious Earl," I explained. "We've been looking for a piece of, well, it's not pure uranium, it's actually pitchblende, which is a rock. And half of Mrs. Cooper's rock went missing and we're looking for it."

"You said a rock?" Earl asked.

"Yes," Kimberly responded. "It's about yay big," Kimberly used her hands to demonstrate its size.

"Hmm," Earl said, deep in thought. "I do remember something."

"Yes?" Andrea asked.

"Well, you can't tell anyone but..." Earl began. "A few weeks before the start of school I was cleaning up in Mrs. Cooper's back room. She never wants me cleaning back there. In fact, she has a sign on the door that says 'Do Not Clean.' But, if you knew how dirty it got back there, you'd understand that every now and then I gotta clean. So before the teachers returned to school I went back there and did some tidying up. Phew, was it dirty. And, well, in my tidying up, I did by accident knock over a box, and a rock came out. So I put the rock back inside the box and returned it to the shelf."

"What kind of box?" I asked Earl, thinking that we had stumbled upon our 'culprit.'

"It wasn't nothing special. Just a metal box."

"Could you show it to us?" I asked.

"Yeah, show it to us, please Earl," Kimberly added.

"Please!" Andrea said.

Earl looked over his shoulder at the approaching men in black and said, "Yes, but quickly. Mrs. Cooper would have my hide if she knew I was letting you into her back room. She'd have my hide if she knew what I had done," he said. He motioned for us to join him. Alex came along.

He grabbed a key from the retractable cable attached to his belt, and opened Mrs. Cooper's room. He held the door open for us.

We all went in. Earl followed us in, shut the door behind us, and proceeded to the storeroom. He looked behind him to the right and left, nervous about being caught, and retrieved another key from his belt. He opened the storeroom, but this time he went in first. We followed behind him, whether we were allowed to or not. Earl looked for the box he had dropped but didn't see it where he had left it.

"It doesn't seem to be here," he muttered as he continued looking on nearby shelves. Then he noticed it laying on the table in front of him. "This is it, right here."

"That's the box!" I exclaimed. "You said that you dropped it but put the rock back inside."

"Yes," said Earl.

"What happened to the other half?" I asked.

"There wasn't anymore... at least," Earl thought to himself. "At least, not that I was aware of."

"Where did you drop it? Do you remember?" Kimberly asked.

"Well, if I remember correctly," Earl said, "It was up on this shelf," indicating the second shelf above the table. "I lifted it up to clean behind it, and it fell right outta my hand." Earl paused, thinking. "It landed somewhere around there," he pointed to an area of floor to the left of us.

"You're saying it was uranium?" Earl asked, now more concerned about the implication of what he had handled, what he had exposed himself to, and what he had dropped.

"Well, let's find out," I said. I took my backpack off my shoulder, opened its front pocket to get my mom's Geiger counter. I turned it on and heard the characteristic random clicking. I brought it to the lead-lined box and didn't notice any significant increase in noise and then decided to sweep the room with it, starting with the floor. Everyone else backed away, more comfortable with looking on from a distance. I guess they had learned their lesson about shielding well.

I brought the counter down to where Earl said he had dropped the uranium and the clicking sound accelerated. I moved the Geiger counter around and inched myself in the direction of the increasing sound. I followed it toward the sink at the one end of the room. It was telling me I was getting close. I got down on my hands and knees and moved the Geiger counter around until I landed on the source of the sound — the other half of the pitchblende rock!

"I think we found the culprit!" I exclaimed. I turned off the Geiger counter, got back to my feet and picked up the gloves lying next to the box that Mrs. Cooper had used to show the pitchblende to the class.

I put the gloves on, picked up the pitchblende and returned it to the lead-lined box on the table, after which I returned the gloves to the table.

"Operation Uranium accomplished!" I said. "Now, let's get out of here!" I said. "Remember, proximity and time of exposure!"

We all scrambled out of the storeroom and Earl locked the door behind us.

"I never realized that there was something so dangerous back here. I should have listened to Mrs. Cooper," Earl said. "Now I don't know what's going to happen to me, either from the exposure, or from Mrs. Cooper."

"Don't worry Earl, we'll cover for you," I said.

"Yeah," the girls agreed.

Only Alex remained silent.

"Alex?!" I said.

"Yeah," he said reluctantly. "But, could I just get one picture?" he asked.

"No!" said the rest of us in unison.

"And, as far as exposure Earl, don't worry too much about it. We're all exposed to radioactivity. Cosmic rays from the universe fall on us all the time. What matters is..."

"Proximity and time of exposure!" Andrea, Kimberly, and I said in unison.

"But what are you going to say to Mrs. Cooper?" Earl asked.

"We'll think of something," I said.

At that moment, a man in black entered Mrs. Cooper's room and told us to evacuate the building. As our work here was done, we obeyed. Besides, I didn't know about Andrea and Kimberly, but I was starving.

The four of us (yes, Alex too) went home by way of Pete's ice cream shop. We ate our ice cream at one of the tables out in front and reminisced about our adventures that day, the "found" uranium, and discussed the President's visit tomorrow, that each of us was going to miss — all but Alex. Finding the missing uranium cost us a high price. But it was worth it to have Kimberly back as a friend.

Alex was already making a pest of himself taking pictures of the popular kids eating their ice cream, which annoyed them to no end. I tried to pretend that he wasn't with us, but alas, it was obvious that he was. I shrugged my shoulders to them, as if to say, "What can I do?" and went back to my ice cream, mint chocolate chip shake -- the usual.

29

The Real Final Project

I entered science class the next day, excited to tell Mrs. Cooper about our findings. Usually, Kimberly was there before me. But today she wasn't. In fact, neither was Mrs. Cooper. The two of them entered the classroom just before the tardy bell, seemingly deep in conversation. I thought we had agreed that we would present our findings to Mrs. Cooper together, but it seems as if Kimberly was back to her old tricks, dismissing me and taking all the credit for herself.

When they finished talking, Kimberly sat herself down at our table.

"What were you two talking about?" I whispered.

"Nothing," Kimberly whispered back.

That wasn't a great answer, but Mrs. Cooper was starting class.

"Class, remember that we have an assembly sixth period today."

"In which you're going to be named 'Teacher of the Year,'" Nick blurted out.

"Yes Nick, that's right. I just wanted to give you a heads up that I will be leaving class early to get ready, and you'll have a sub for the rest of the period.

"Yay!" said a boy in the corner.

"No!" said most of the rest of us.

"I need to know," I whispered even more loudly to Kimberly. "What were you two talking about?"

"Nothing!"

"It wasn't nothing," I said to her under my breath.

"You'll see," Kimberly said. "It's good, don't worry."

It's good, don't worry. I let those words sink in, but the truth was, I was worried.

"Before I go, I was told that Kimberly and Sam have a second part to their project they wanted to present to the class. If that's okay with you class, we'll let them go first."

Kimberly and I walked to the front of the class. Luckily, Andrea had arrived to join us just in time. She had gotten permission from her fifth period teacher.

"Yesterday, we presented a model of a uranium atom that decayed into thorium by giving off an alpha particle, and then into protactinium, by giving off a beta particle," I began.

$$^{238}_{92}\text{U} \rightarrow {}^{234}_{90}\text{Th}^+ {}^{4}_{2}\text{He} \rightarrow {}^{234}_{91}\text{Pa}^+ {}^{0}_{-1}\text{e}$$

green   red   alpha particle   blue

"Today, we are presenting a real uranium atom. Well, actually billions of uranium atoms."

"Heh?" Diego commented.

Kimberly took her cue and retrieved the lead box of pitchblende from the back room.

"Mrs. Cooper, allow us to present the missing uranium!"

Many students got up from their seats and inched closer to see.

Kimberly put on Mrs. Cooper's lead-lined gloves, opened the box, and presented the two halves of the uranium for all to see.

"My pitchblende!" Mrs. Cooper exclaimed. "Where did you find it?"

"It had been very close by all along," Kimberly exclaimed. "But it took a crack set of girl scientists to sleuth it out. Sam, Andrea and me."

With that, I turned on the museum's Geiger counter, held it over the two reunited pieces of pitchblende and listened to the clicking go wild.

I turned off the Geiger counter, Kimberly closed the box again, and I explained.

"You see, Mrs. Cooper," I said. "We first didn't know how to find a missing rock, because, well to be honest, there were many rocks on campus. So we got the idea to borrow a Geiger counter from my mom's work." I held up the Geiger counter to show everyone.

"When we brought the Geiger counter to school, we quickly learned there was radiation everywhere."

"Everywhere," Andrea repeated for emphasis.

"We figured out we needed to protect ourselves. So we designed hazmat suits out of whatever odds and ends we had at home. Of course, lead, the best way to shield against radiation, was hard to come by."

"So we made due," said Kimberly.

"So we made due," I repeated. "Then, you taught us that of course radiation is all around us, that it came from the Big Bang and that there's even radioactive isotopes in our bodies. So we got a little less scared. But we weren't exactly relieved to find this out.

"Once we got over that initial shock, we used the Geiger counter to lead us to the missing uranium. It seemed to be leading us to Mr. Phillips's office. When we saw him talking with the men in black, we were sure that Mr. Phillips was in on the whole thing and that there was a uranium smuggling operation going on at Taft Middle School right under our noses.

"It turns out, however, that the men in black were simply the Secret Service here preparing for the President's visit."

"And not part of an international smuggling ring," Andrea interjected.

"And not part of an international smuggling ring," I repeated.

"We didn't find the missing uranium in Mr. Phillips's office, even though something in his office did set off the Geiger counter. But I got caught before I could find the source. And, well, needless to say we got into a lot of trouble. And because of that, we won't be able to go to the assembly and meet the President."

"And, on top of that," Andrea added, "I agreed to paint a portrait of Mr. Phillips, which is going to be a very sad portrait indeed."

"And then we set up a trap to catch the smugglers, by advertising in the school announcements that we had the other rock to give them. They were supposed to meet us after school on the playground."

"And, well, no one showed up..."

"Except for Earl," Kimberly chimed in. I gave her a look that said, *Remember not to bring Earl into this!*

"We begged Earl to let us look around your chemical storage room for the missing piece," Kimberly added, trying to take the blame off Earl.

"Please don't blame Earl for letting us in. We practically forced him to do so," I added.

"And sure enough," I continued, "the Geiger counter led us to the missing piece on the floor, not far from the box where it came from!"

"So we returned it to its box, and now I'd say, Mrs. Cooper, that this case is now closed," I said.

"Well, I'd definitely say it's closed," Mrs. Cooper said. "Except for a couple of loose ends."

"Earl came to me first thing this morning and admitted that he had dropped the uranium rock and that it had broken in two. He was just sick about it."

The three of us looked at each other.

"It's ok. Earl's not in trouble. Accidents happen. And, well, I should get the back room cleaned once in a while."

"And, you told me that the principal's office was setting off the Geiger counter, which causes me concern," Mrs. Cooper continued.

"Yes, but we couldn't find the source of the uranium in his office. So the jury's still out," I said.

"Hmm," Mrs. Cooper said as she thought to herself.

"And now, Kimberly missed her cheerleading practice, so she lost her chance of becoming head cheerleader," I said.

"And Andrea missed her callbacks, so she didn't get into the Madrigals," Kimberly added.

Just then, Mr. Phillips walked in with the substitute teacher.

"It's time to go Mrs. Cooper," he said.

"One second Mr. Phillips. Sam, do you still have that Geiger counter on you?"

"Yes I do," I said, holding up the counter.

"Please turn it on," she instructed.

I did just what Mrs. Cooper told me to do.

"Bring the Geiger counter toward Mr. Phillips. Mr. Phillips, you don't mind, do you?" Mrs. Cooper asked.

"I, uh," he didn't know how to respond in that split second in front of the students.

I waved the Geiger counter around the principal, and sure enough it sounded off uncontrollably the closer it got to him.

"That's enough Sam. Turn it off," Mrs. Cooper said.

"Mr. Phillips, what do you know about your watch?" Mrs. Cooper asked.

"Why, it was my grandfather's watch. My father handed it down to me at my college graduation. The dial glows in the dark even without exposing it to sunlight!" He brought his watch-bearing wrist closer to Mrs. Cooper.

"Yes, I'm sure it does," Mrs. Cooper said.

"Did you know that many watches from the early part of the twentieth were painted with radium paint, a highly radioactive material? That's what gives it its phosphorescence - which means its ability to glow in the dark, even without being exposed to light. You shouldn't be wearing that watch, however. It gives off a lot of alpha particles. And the two factors that can keep you safe from radioactivity are —"

"Proximity and length of exposure!" The three of us chanted in unison.

"Oh wow," Mr. Phillips said. "I didn't know." He took off the watch.

"For now, I'll put it in my lead-lined box, until you figure out what you want to do with it," said Mrs. Cooper.

Mr. Phillips handed over the watch.

"Now that that's settled, we need to hurry over to the assembly. Even without my watch, I know we're late," Mr. Phillips said.

"Yes, it's time... but not without Sam Gold, the scientist who solved the mystery of the missing uranium!"

"Me?" I said.

"Yes," Mrs. Cooper responded. "Kimberly told me how much you did to help clear her name and prove she wasn't responsible. And I believe that the President of the United States should meet a budding young scientist like you!"

"Is that what you were talking about when you walked in with Mrs. Cooper?" I asked Kimberly.

Kimberly nodded her head.

"Ok, then bring Sam too. Let's just go," Mr. Phillips said impatiently.

"Not without Kimberly and Andrea!" I interjected. "I wouldn't have been able to find the uranium without them."

"Fine, fine, bring them too," Mr. Phillips said. "I just don't want us to be late!"

As the five of us walked quickly to the auditorium, we were talking about what we'd say to the President if we were introduced to him.

When we actually got the chance — and we did — I was a lot more tongue-tied than I'd thought I would be.

30

Hail to the Chief

Mr. Phillips introduced Mrs. Cooper to the President first, and then Mrs. Cooper introduced each one of us, one at a time.

"Ms. Newhouse," he said to Kimberly. "I hear you missed your cheerleading practice to help make Taft Middle School safe for all of its students, teachers and staff. You are a true hero. Would you mind starting today's assembly with your favorite cheerleading routine?"

Kimberly didn't know what to say.

And to Andrea he said, "I hear that you're an artist."

Oh no, I thought to myself. He's going to want her to paint his picture too!

"Not so much a visual artist, but a singer, is that right?"

"Y-yes!" said Andrea.

"Would you do me the honor of leading the assembly by chanting the National Anthem?"

"Really?!" Andrea was overjoyed. "Yes!"

"Ms. Gold" the President said to me. "I hear you're a good friend, and a super young scientist. Keep up the good work. We need more scientists like you," the President said to me.

And so that's how it happened. That's how three girls saved Taft Middle School from uranium exposure and met the President of the United States. One got to dance, one got to sing, and one well, one did what she always wanted to do — S.C.I.E.N.C.E.

* * *

As I went to shake the President's hand, my Geiger counter chose the most inopportune time to go off. Especially since I thought I *had* turned it off earlier.

I sure wish I had.

What could I do? The closer I got to the President, the louder it clicked. I couldn't just ignore his extended hand. I looked up at the Secret Service sheepishly.

Then I looked at the President apologetically and shrugged my shoulders. Here goes nothing.

I returned his handshake, and glanced at his wrist, certain that he too had a radium dial on his watch. Except that he wasn't wearing a watch. My Geiger counter couldn't be wrong. How would I tell the President of the United States that he is, well, radioactive?

THE REAL FINAL PROJECT

Rocket Girls

The Science Behind It

The Science Behind It

By the end of the 1800s, scientists (especially physicists) had believed they had discovered everything about the known world. So much so, that the scientist Lord Kelvin is quoted as saying to the British Association for the Advancement of Science, "There is nothing new to be discovered in physics now. All that remains is more and more precise measurement."

He was very, very wrong. But, there's no evidence that he actually said this.

The Discovery of Radioactivity

If he had, it would have been around the same time that Wilhelm Conrad Roentgen, a German physicist, discovered X-rays -- 1895. Which seems to show that there were more things to be discovered in physics after all.

You've seen x-rays, or at least x-ray machines. And you know that they can be used to look inside people to see their bones, teeth, and even lungs.

X-rays are a form of electromagnetic radiation, also known as light. Light is a wave that moves at the very fast speed of 3.8 million meters per second. Light is more than what happens when you turn a lamp on. The light that you see with your eyes is called visible light. Visible light is only one small part of all light.

Electromagnetic Spectrum

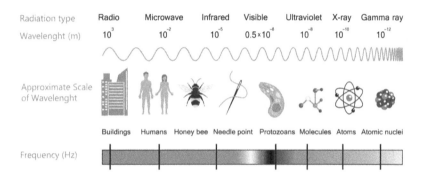

Radiation type	Radio	Microwave	Infrared	Visible	Ultraviolet	X-ray	Gamma ray
Wavelenght (m)	10^3	10^{-2}	10^{-5}	0.5×10^{-6}	10^{-8}	10^{-10}	10^{-12}

Approximate Scale of Wavelenght

| Buildings | Humans | Honey bee | Needle point | Protozoans | Molecules | Atoms | Atomic nuclei |

Frequency (Hz)

Visible light has a wavelength between 380 to 740 nanometers. A nanometer is a billionth of a meter. We could say 380 billionth of a meter, but scientists prefer numbers that are easier to say. Visible light can be further broken down into the colors of the rainbow — red, orange, yellow, blue, indigo, and violet (ROYGBIV). The longest wavelength of visible light is red, and the shortest wavelength of visible light is violet.

A wavelength is the distance between two peaks in a wave.

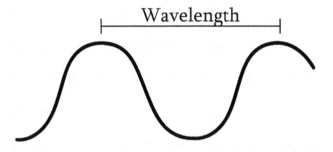

Waves are a form of energy. You've most likely seen ocean waves. Ocean waves are the result of energy moving through the water. When you throw a rock in a pond, you can see its ripple effects in the water. These ripples are waves of energy that the moving rock gives to the water. The more energy the rock has, the more energy is transmitted to the water. Heavier and faster moving rocks have more energy than smaller, slower moving rocks.

The shorter the wavelength, the higher the energy of the wave. Light waves with longer wavelengths and less energy than visible light are infrared, microwave, and radio waves. Light waves with shorter wavelengths and higher energy than visible light are ultraviolet, X-rays, and gamma rays. Some animals can see ultraviolet ("above violet") waves, like reindeer, owls, and salmon.

As soon as Roentgen's discovery of high energy waves known as x-rays spread throughout Europe, Henri Becquerel in France wondered if there was a connection between these newly discovered x-rays and the phosphorescence of uranium salts. He had inherited a supply of phosphorescent uranium salts from his father. Being a fourth-generation physicist, this wasn't far-fetched. Becquerel supposed that these phosphorescent uranium salts absorbed lower energy visible light from the sun and emitted this light as x-rays.

To test his theory, he covered photographic plates with black paper so that they would not be able to absorb sunlight. He placed uranium salt on top of these covered plates and left them out in the sun. When he later unwrapped the black paper, he saw the outlines of the salt on the photographic plate. As the plates themselves were blocked from sunlight, the outlines of the salt must be due to x-rays given off by the uranium.

Like any good scientist, he wanted to test his conclusion. But, the weather being cloudy for the next few days, he placed the plate and the uranium salt inside his desk drawer and waited for the sunlight to reemerge. For some reason that no one seems to know for sure, he developed the plates that he had left in his drawer. And what did he find? The uranium salts had left a crystal clear image on the photographic plate without any sunlight at all! In other words, there must be light coming from within the uranium salts that did not come from sunlight.

He later found out that he could achieve the same results with uranium salts that were not phosphorescent. Clearly all uranium salts produced light. And, the light that came from uranium was discovered not to be x-rays because it could be bent by electric and magnetic fields. X-rays cannot be bent because they are neutral - they have no charge. Instead of discovering a new source of x-rays, Henri Becquerel discovered radioactivity.

The Discovery of the Atom and Its Subatomic Particles

Roughly 100 years earlier, in 1803, John Dalton, a British schoolteacher, came up with his Atomic Theory to explain the observable phenomena of his day. He proposed that all matter was made up of tiny indivisible particles known as atoms.

To be honest, this wasn't a new theory. In fact, it was first proposed by a Greek philosopher named Democritus who was born around 460 BCE (before the Common Era - before the year zero). Democritus imagined that if you kept dividing matter repeatedly, you'd eventually reach a point where you couldn't divide it anymore. He called that point *atomos* which is Greek for "indivisible." Democritus' theory did not catch on, as he was less influential than Aristotle who believed that matter was made up of earth, water, air, and fire.

Still all those years later, the idea of the atom was in the back of scientists' minds.

Dalton, without having the tools to prove his theory, was surprisingly close to what we know about atoms today. The most significant changes to his theory, however, took place in the 1900s, around the same time as x-rays and radioactivity.

The Atom IS Divisible

Electrons

In 1896, a British physicist named J.J. Thomson discovered that a cathode ray could be deflected by electrically charged plates. A cathode ray is a beam emitted from the cathode of a tube after all the air is pumped out. When all the air is pumped out, it's referred to as a vacuum. A vacuum is not a vacuum cleaner, but it is related. Vacuum cleaners work by sucking out the air, which creates a negative pressure. Since the air pressure outside of the vacuum is greater than the air pressure inside the vacuum, the air (and all the dirty around it) is sucked into the vacuum.

An example you may be more familiar with is drinking from a straw. When you drink from a straw, your mouth creates negative pressure around the straw, so that the contents of your drink, which are under greater pressure than your mouth, get sucked up.

Back to the cathode ray. The cathode ray is a vacuum tube, meaning all the air inside has been pumped out. No one at the time knew what these cathode rays were made of until J.J. Thomson started experimenting with them.

He applied both a positively-charged plate to the tube and a negatively-charged plate. He saw that the cathode ray beam bent away from the negative plate and toward the positive plate. Since opposite charges attract (positive and negative are attracted to each other), Thomson knew that the beam consisted of negative particles. He called these negative particles corpuscles. Today we call them electrons. Since electrons are contained inside the atom, the atom is NOT the smallest particle of matter.

J.J. Thomson, knowing that the atom overall was neutral, meaning it has no charge, believed that the atom contained positive charge as well, but he never could find it. Using what he knew and discovered about the atom, he came up with the Plum Pudding Model. In the Plum Pudding Model, the plums represent the negatively-charged electrons, and the pudding represents the positive stuff.

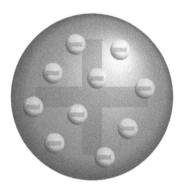

Thomson's Plum Pudding Model of the Atom

The Nucleus

Ernest Rutherford was a New Zealand scientist who, along with his lab students Geiger and Marsden, performed many experiments with radioactivity. He was eventually awarded the Nobel prize for discovering alpha and beta decay, the giving off of alpha and beta particles from an atom. One would think this was enough of a discovery for one lifetime. However, he had one more discovery up his sleeve that made him even more famous.

Having already discovered that uranium gave off alpha particles, which were particles made up of 2 protons and 2 neutrons, Rutherford set up an experiment in which he shot alpha particles at a piece of gold foil, no more than a few atoms thick. Once the alpha particles went through the gold foil, they would make a bright green flash on the screen behind it. Most of the time, the alpha particles he shot at the gold foil went straight through and hit the back screen. Sometimes, the alpha particle was deflected a little by the gold foil, and hit the back screen at an angle. And once in a very long while, an alpha particle would hit the gold foil, and bounce back right at the source.

Rutherford exclaimed, "It was quite the most incredible event that has ever happened to me in my life. It was almost as incredible as if you fired a 15-inch shell at a piece of tissue paper and it came back and hit you."

Why was Rutherford so surprised? Remember that alpha particles are positively-charged. Rutherford believed, as did all scientists at the time, that the atom was like Thomson's Plum Pudding model. The negative charges were randomly located inside the plum pudding, and the positive stuff was spread throughout. We've already learned that opposite charges attract. It is also true that like charges repel each other. The thing was, there wasn't enough positive charge in any one place to repel the alpha particle with enough force to bounce back to the source. He had to come up with another model.

Rutherford proposed that the positive charge in an atom was not spread throughout, but was located in a small dense area. When an alpha particle hit this positively-charged dense area, it would bounce off it, depending on the angle with which it hit it. However, since these positively-charged areas were so small compared to the size of the gold foil, they were only hit once in a while.

Rutherford called the positively-charged center of an atom its nucleus. The nucleus gets its positive charge because it contains the positively-charged protons.

Along with the protons in the nucleus are often neutrons which have the same mass as protons but have no charge (neutral).

The Periodic Table

Long before protons and the nucleus were discovered, a Russian chemistry teacher Dmitri Mendeleev created the Periodic Table. The Periodic Table is a table of all the known elements arranged in order of repeating chemical properties. For example, when he arranged the atoms in order of increasing atomic mass, he found that sodium (Na) reacted with the same elements as did lithium (Li), so he put Na in the same column as Li.

This is like arranging cards from a card deck. If you put all the Ace's together in this order — hearts, diamonds, clubs, and spades - and two's, and three's and so on, you'd lay out the first row like this:

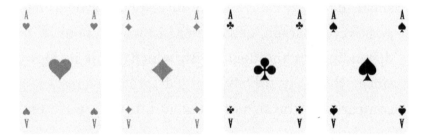

Your next card would be the two of hearts. You could put the two of hearts to the right of the Ace of spades. But, noticing that the two of hearts is like the Ace of hearts because they are of the same suit, Mendeleev would have added the two of hearts to the heart's column below the Ace of hearts, and do the same with the two of diamonds, two of clubs, and two of spades.

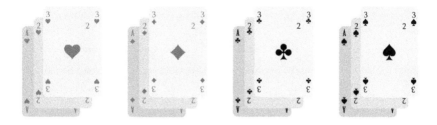

The similar property of suit — hearts, diamonds, clubs, and spades — repeats every fifth card.

Once Rutherford discovered the nucleus and the protons inside it, scientists were able to improve on Mendeleev's Periodic Table. Whereas Mendeleev arranged the Periodic Table by atomic mass, scientists found that, if they arranged the Periodic Table by atomic number -- the number of protons in the nucleus of an atom -- it worked even better.

Every atom is defined by the number of protons in its nucleus. If it has only one proton, then the atom is hydrogen – element #1 on the Periodic Table. Hydrogen has an atomic number of 1, meaning it has 1 proton. Every helium atom has two protons in its nucleus. And so on.

The Modern Periodic Table is a little different, therefore, from Mendeleev's original Periodic Table. Mendeleev ordered the elements by atomic mass because protons had yet to be discovered. The Modern Periodic Table is arranged by atomic number.

Chemical Reactions

Chemical reactions, such as an explosion, or forming rust on metal, or creating a baking soda volcano, happen when electrons are exchanged between atoms. For example, the formation of rust is the reaction between iron and oxygen in the atmosphere, forming iron oxide:

$$4\,Fe + 3\,O_2 \rightarrow 2\,Fe_2O_3$$

In chemical reactions, atoms are rearranged but they're never changed into other atoms.

In the above example, we start with 4 iron (Fe) atoms, and we end with 4 iron (Fe) atoms. On the reactant side (the left-hand side of the equation), we have 4 Fe. On the product side (the right-hand side of the equation), we have 4 Fe as well, but they're bonded to oxygen to form rust as follows: 2 Fe_2O_3. In the compound 2 Fe_2O_3, there are still 4 iron (Fe) atoms (and 6 oxygen (O) atoms).

Nuclide Symbols

In addition to the atomic number, which is the number of protons in an atom, there is another important number called the mass number. The mass number is the number of protons plus the number of neutrons in the nucleus of an atom. The number of neutrons has nothing to do with the identity of the atom. You can have three atoms of hydrogen, each with a different number of neutrons. However, every hydrogen atom in the universe has only one proton. We say, therefore, that hydrogen has an atomic number of 1. Most hydrogen atoms have zero neutrons, which makes their mass number equal to 1 as well.

$$\text{mass number} = \text{number of protons} + \text{number of neutrons}$$
$$\text{mass number} = \quad\quad 1 \quad\quad + \quad\quad 0 \quad = 1$$

Some atoms of hydrogen, though far fewer, have one neutron. Hydrogen atoms with one neutron are sometimes called deuterium because they have a mass number of 2.

$$\text{mass number} = \text{number of protons} + \text{number of neutrons}$$
$$\text{mass number} = \quad\quad 1 \quad\quad + \quad\quad 1 \quad\quad = 2$$

And much rarer are hydrogen atoms with two neutrons. They are known as tritium because they have a mass number of 3.

$$\text{mass number} = \text{number of protons} + \text{number of neutrons}$$
$$\text{mass number} = \quad\quad 1 \quad\quad + \quad\quad 2 \quad\quad = 3$$

A nuclide symbol is a way of writing an element that provides both its atomic number and mass number.

These are the nuclide symbols for H-1, H-2, and H-3, respectively. (By the way, when an element's symbol is hyphenated to a number, that number is the mass number.)

$$^{1}_{1}\text{H} \quad\quad ^{2}_{1}\text{H} \quad\quad ^{3}_{1}\text{H}$$

H-1, H-2, and H-3 are isotopes of each other. Isotopes are two or more atoms of the same element with different mass numbers.

Here would be the nuclide symbols for uranium-235 and uranium-238. (Again, 235 and 238 are mass numbers. All uranium atoms contain 92 protons).

$$^{235}_{92}U \quad ^{238}_{92}U$$

U-235 and U-238 are isotopes of each other. The isotope U-235 can undergo nuclear fission, which is a process in which it splits in half and releases a tremendous amount of energy. An atom that can split in two is said to be fissile (derived from the term fission). The first atomic bomb was made from U-235. U-238, on the other hand, is not fissile.

Radioactivity (Nuclear Reactions)

A radioactive atom is an atom that is unstable because it either has too many protons and neutrons in its nucleus, or an unstable ratio of protons to neutrons. A radioactive atom tries to become stable by getting rid of particles from the nucleus. These particles can be alpha particles, which consist of two protons and two neutrons, beta particles which are like electrons, or positrons, which are positively-charged electrons.

There is a lot of energy in the nucleus of an atom, so high energy radiation is often given off along with these particles.

Alpha Decay

Alpha decay is the giving off of alpha particles from the nucleus of an unstable atom. An alpha particle consists of two protons and two neutrons.

When a nucleus gives off an alpha particle, it changes into an atom with two fewer protons and two fewer neutrons.

Oftentimes, an alpha particle is written as helium, because helium's nucleus contains 2 protons and 2 neutrons.

For example, when uranium-238 gives off an alpha particle, it becomes thorium-234 as follows:

$$^{238}_{92}U \longrightarrow {}^{234}_{90}Th + {}^{4}_{2}He$$

U-238 in this example is referred to as the parent nuclide and Th-234 is the daughter nuclide.

Notice how the sum of the mass numbers of the decay products Th-234 and He-4 add up to the mass number of U-238. Also notice how the atomic numbers of Th-234 (90) and He-4 (2) add up to the atomic number of U-238 (92).

Beta Decay

Beta decay is the giving off of a beta particle from the nucleus of an unstable atom. A beta particle is just like an electron in mass and charge. The difference between a beta particle and an electron is that electrons are always outside an atom's nucleus, whereas a beta particle comes from within an atom's nucleus.

A beta particle is formed when a neutron, which has no charge, splits apart into a positively charged and negatively charged particle. The positively-charged particle it becomes is a proton. The negatively-charged particle is a beta particle.

Therefore, when a beta particle is given off, it causes a neutron to turn into a proton, which increases its atomic number by one. Because the total number of protons plus neutrons doesn't change, the mass number stays the same.

Thorium-234, the daughter nuclide of uranium-238, is itself unstable and undergoes beta decay.

$$^{234}_{90}\text{Th} \rightarrow\ ^{234}_{91}\text{Pa} +\ ^{0}_{-1}\text{e}$$

The daughter nuclide of Thorium-234 contains one more proton that its parent. This is because a neutron turned into a proton, releasing a beta particle.

Notice how the sum of the mass numbers of the decay products Pa-234 and e-0 add up to the mass number of Th-234. Also notice how the atomic numbers of Pa-234 (91) and e-0 (-1) add up to the atomic number of Th-234 (90).

Positron Decay

Some unstable nuclei decay by emitting a positron. A positron is a positively-charged beta particle in the nucleus of an atom.

A positron is formed when a proton, which has a positive charge, splits apart into a neutral particle and a positively-charged particle. The neutral particle it becomes is a neutron. The positively-charged particle is a positron.

Therefore, when a positron is given off, it causes a proton to turn into a neutron, which decreases its atomic number by one. Because the total number of protons plus neutrons doesn't change, the mass number stays the same.

The radioactive isotope O-15 undergoes positron decay to become N-15.

$$^{15}_{8}O \rightarrow ^{15}_{7}N + ^{0}_{1}e^{+}$$

Notice how the sum of the mass numbers of the decay products N-15 and e-0 add up to the mass number of O-15. Also notice how the atomic numbers of N-15 (7) and e-0 (+1) add up to the atomic number of O-15 (8).

Gamma Decay

Gamma decay is different from the previous types of radioactive decay. In gamma decay, a particle is not given off by the nucleus, so the atom's identity doesn't change. In gamma decay, gamma radiation is given off. Gamma decay often accompanies other types of decay, like alpha, beta, or positron decay.

Gamma radiation is a form of electromagnetic radiation, just as x-rays are. Gamma waves are more energetic than even x-rays. They are the most penetrating form of radioactivity.

Electromagnetic Spectrum

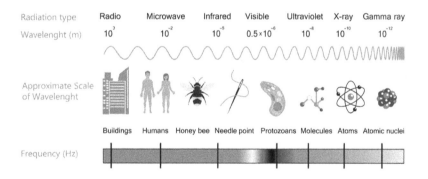

Background Radiation

Background radiation refers to the natural radiation you're exposed to on a regular basis. Background radiation consists of cosmic radiation from the universe, the radiation from naturally occurring radioactive isotopes, as well as the radiation from x-rays, and nuclear events such as nuclear weapons and nuclear accidents.

Shielding

You will most likely never be exposed to any radioactivity beyond background radioactivity. If you were exposed to an abundance of radiation, you should protect yourself through shielding, keep your distance, and limit time of exposure.

Shielding refers to blocking the radiation from reaching you. Alpha radiation is blocked by your own skin, as well as by thin materials such as paper.

Beta radiation is blocked by wood and aluminum.

Gamma radiation is blocked by thick lead.

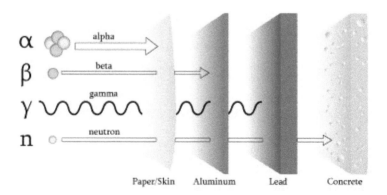

You should distance yourself from any source of radioactivity and limit your time of exposure.

Half-Lives

Radioactive decay is measured in half-lives. A half-life is the time it takes for half of a radioactive sample to decay into its daughter nuclei. Different radioactive isotopes have different half-lives.

If you started with 12 grams of a radioactive isotope, it would take one half-life for half of it to decay into its daughter nuclei. If its half-life were 2 days, then, at the end of 2 days, 6 grams of the radioactive sample would remain, and 6 grams would have decayed. It would take another half-life, for half of the remaining 6 grams of radioactive isotope to decay into its daughter nuclei. It would take a third half-life for half of the remaining 3 grams of radioactive isotope to decay into its daughter nuclei. Since each half-life is 2 days, three half-lives would take 6 days.

$$12_g \xrightarrow{\text{2 days}} 6_g \xrightarrow{\text{2 days}} 3_g \xrightarrow{\text{2 days}} 1.5_g \xrightarrow{\text{2 days}} 0.75_g \xrightarrow{\text{2 days}}$$

Carbon-14 is an isotope that is used to measure how old a fossil is. C-14 has a half-life of 5,730 years. As long as an organism is living, it absorbs carbon, a small percentage of which is C-14. Once it dies, it no longer absorbs carbon. By measuring how much C-14 has decayed in a fossil, scientists can determine its age. For instance, if it contains 50% less C-14 than a living species, then one half-life has probably passed. That sample would be roughly 5,730 years old. If it contains 75% less C-14 than a living species, then two half-lives have probably passed. That sample would be roughly two times 5,730 years old, or 11,460 years old.

Rocket Girls

Science Experiments and Activities

Make a Cloud Chamber

Introduction

A cloud chamber allows you to see the tracks of radioactive particles.

Materials

- Petri dish
- Black construction paper, one sheet
- sticky-back black felt
- radiation source (Pb-210 needle) (website: https://www.spectrumtechniques.com/)
- isopropyl alcohol (91% or higher)
- dry ice (available in many grocery stores)
- gloves to handle the dry ice
- flashlight
- Caution
- Do this experiment with a responsible adult.

- You will need an adult to purchase the radioactive source.
- Handle the dry ice with gloves.
- Do NOT touch the needle of the radioactive source. Store in a safe place.
- 91% and higher isopropyl alcohol is very flammable. Read the MSDS guidelines before handling.

Procedure

1. Cut a circle out of the black construction paper that will fit neatly inside your petri dish.
2. Cut a piece of black felt that will cover the inside rim/edges of the petri dish.
3. Place the black construction paper inside the petri dish.
4. Adhere the black felt to the inside rim of the petri dish.
5. Soak your felt with the isopropyl alcohol.
6. Place your radiation source inside the petri dish.
7. Place the lid on top.
8. Hold the petri dish between your hands for a moment to warm it up. This will help the isopropyl alcohol to start evaporating.
9. Place the petri dish on top of the dry ice.
10. Turn off the lights.
11. Shine the flashlight into your chamber from the sides.

12. Watch for the motion of radioactive particles!

The Science Behind It

The cloud inside the petri dish is caused by the evaporation of isopropyl alcohol. Once the vapor particles fall toward the dry ice, they condense back into liquid particles. The cloud is formed from the continual vaporization and condensation of the alcohol particles.

Lead-210 decays by beta decay. What you're seeing in the cloud chamber however are the short, dense tracks of alpha particles. Why alpha particles?

Lead-210 undergoes beta decay to produce bismuth-210.

$$^{210}_{82}\text{Pb} \longrightarrow {}^{210}_{83}\text{Bi} + {}^{0}_{-1}\text{e}$$

Bismuth-210 undergoes beta decay to produce polonium-210.

$$^{210}_{83}\text{Bi} \longrightarrow {}^{210}_{84}\text{Po} + {}^{0}_{-1}\text{e}$$

Polonium-210 undergoes alpha decay to produce lead-206. This is the source of the alpha particles.

As these positively-charged alpha particles leave the radiation source, they travel through the clouds and ionize the alcohol vapor. The alcohol vapor then condenses where those tracks were.

Source:
https://education.jlab.org/frost/cloud_chamber.html

Half-Life of Candium

Introduction

A half-life is the amount of time it takes for half of a sample of undecayed atoms to decay. In this experiment, you will be drawing the decay curve of the isotope "Candium," using M&Ms (or similar candy that has writing on one side. You could also use pennies — pennies landing heads-down have "decayed").

Materials

- 1.69 oz Bag of M&M's (More than one if you want to do the extension activities)
- Ziplock bag
- Graph paper

Procedure

1. Open the bag of M&Ms and count them. Record this number in the table as the number of undecayed atoms at zero half-lives.

Number of Half-Lives	Remaining (Undecayed) Atoms

2.   Place the M&Ms inside the Ziploc bag and seal it.

3.   Gently shake for 10 seconds.

4.   Gently pour out candy and count the number of pieces with the print side down.

5.   Record the data: These atoms have "decayed."

6.   Return only the pieces with the print side up to the bag and reseal it.

7.   Consume the "decayed atoms."

8.   Gently shake the sealed bag for 10 seconds.

9.   Continue shaking, counting, and consuming until all the atoms have decayed.

10. To graph the number of undecayed atoms vs. time on your graph paper, label the x-axis "Time" and number the grids in intervals of 10 seconds (the length of the half-life) from 0 seconds to the total number of half-lives you recorded. (For example, if you recorded 20 half-lives, and each half-life was 10 seconds, then you would number up to 200 seconds).

11. Label the y-axis "Number of Undecayed Atoms" and number the grids starting from zero up to the total number of "atoms" you started with.

12. Plot the data from your table.

13. Draw a curve through the points.

Questions to Answer

1.   What is a half-life?

2.   In the experiment, what was the half-life of the element candium?

3.   At the end of two half-lives, what fraction of the atoms had NOT decayed?

4.   Describe the shape of the curve drawn in step 13.

Extension

1.   Repeat the experiment three more times, starting with 30 atoms, 80 atoms, and 100 atoms of candium. Compare the resulting graphs.

2.   Repeat the experiment using half-lives of 5 seconds, 20 seconds, and 1 minute. Compare the resulting graphs. What effect does the length of the half-life have on the resulting graphs?

Source:

http://teachers.egfi-k12.org/radioactive-decay-lesson/

Half-Life Licorice

Introduction

A half-life is the amount of time it takes for half of a sample of undecayed atoms to decay. In this experiment, you will use licorice to draw the decay curve of an isotope over time. Eating the licorice is required!

Materials

- one piece of licorice
- graph paper
- ruler
- pen, pencil, or marker

Procedure

1. Label the horizontal axis of your graph paper "Time (seconds)" and the vertical axis "Radioactive Licorice (%)." Each square of the horizontal axis should represent 5 seconds. Two squares should therefore represent 10 seconds. Number the horizontal axis in 10-second intervals.

2. Lay your piece of licorice along the vertical axis at time equals zero seconds. Mark the top of the licorice on the vertical axis. Label this point "100%."

3. Every 10 seconds, for a total period of 90 seconds, you will remove one-half of your licorice and set it aside

(or eat it) and place the remaining piece of licorice on the next 10 second mark and mark its current height.

4. You should be doing this 9 times in all (every 10 seconds for 90 seconds).

5. After the 90 seconds have passed, draw a curve through the points.

Questions to Answer

1. Did the licorice ever completely disappear?

2. If you had started with twice as long a piece of licorice, what difference would there be in the graph line you recorded? (To try this, move back to a time minus (-) 10 seconds and imagine how tall the licorice would have been then.

3. What changes when you use a longer piece of licorice?

4. Describe how the graph would be different if you took another piece of licorice of the same size, but you bit it in half and marked it on the graph every 30 seconds instead of every 10 seconds?

Source:

http://nuclearconnect.org/in-the-classroom/for-teachers/activity-licorice-half-life

Make an Electroscope

Introduction

An electroscope measures static electricity, such as the shock you get when you rub your feet on carpet. Objects are charged when they have either too many electrons, or too few.

Materials

- transparent glass jar such as a mason jar.
- small piece of aluminum foil.
- large paper clip (without plastic coating)
- small piece of cardboard
- pencil
- scissors
- tape (preferably insulated)

Caution

- Have an adult help you with the scissors.

Procedure

How to Make the Electroscope

1. Straighten out the paper clip and bend one end into a U-shaped hook.

2.   Trace the mouth of the jar over a piece of cardboard.

3.   Cut out the cardboard circle.

4.   Cut a small hole in the center of the cardboard circle.

5.   Cut out two pieces of aluminum foil in the shape of a pear-shaped diamond. Make the width of the rounded end the size of a penny. These are the leaves of the electroscope.

6.   Pierce a small hole in each of the two pieces of aluminum near the narrow end.

7.   Ball up the rest of the aluminum foil.

8.   Place the straight end of the paper clip through the hole in the cardboard circle.

9.   Attach the two aluminum foil leaves unto the hook end.

10. Lay the cardboard circle on top of the jar so that the hook and leaves end of the paper clip is suspended inside the jar.

11. Poke the remaining balled up aluminum foil on top of the paper clip that protrudes outside of the jar.

12. Tape the cardboard circle to the top of the jar and tape the paper clip in place.

How to Use the Electroscope

1.   Charge a comb by running it through your hair a few times. Then bring the comb near the aluminum ball and watch what happens to the leaves of the electroscope.

2.   Rub a balloon on your hair and then bring it near the aluminum ball.

3.   Rub glass with a wool cloth and bring it near the aluminum ball.

Extension

Run the fun simulation John Travoltage at https://phet.colorado.edu/en/simulation/john-travoltage to see the flow of electrons from the carpet to the foot to the doorknob.

The Science Behind It

Atoms are made of protons, neutrons, and electrons. Protons are positively-charged, neutrons are neutral, and electrons are negatively-charged. Atoms overall are neutral, meaning they have an equal number of positively and negatively-charged particles. In other words, they have equal numbers of protons and electrons. When you run a comb through your hair, or your feet on carpet, the comb (and your feet) acquire a buildup of excess electrons. Because opposite charges attract and like charges repel, these excess electrons repel the electrons in the aluminum ball. The repelled electrons travel down the paper clip to the aluminum leaves. Since both leaves acquire excess negative charge, they repel each other.

Source:

https://www.instructables.com/how-to-make-an-electroscope-easily/

Build an Electroscope

Introduction

Here's another way to build an electroscope.

Electroscopes measure static electric charge. They do not measure radiation directly. Still, electroscopes were initially used to detect radiation before Geiger counters because ionizing radiation can remove electrons from objects, resulting in them acquiring a static charge.

Materials

To make the electroscope:
- aluminum pie pan
- aluminum foil
- styrofoam cup
- glue
- drinking straw
- thread
- masking tape
- pen, marker, or pencil
- plastic ruler

To test the electroscope:
- balloon
- styrofoam plate

- wool fabric
- comb

Procedure

1. Make two holes toward the bottom of the styrofoam cup to fit a straw through.
2. Push a straw through the two holes.
3. Glue the cup upside down to the center of the aluminum pie pan.
4. Cut a piece of thread about 8 inches long and tie a few knots in one end.
5. Cut a 1-inch square piece of aluminum foil and roll it into a ball around the knots on the thread. The ball should be the size of a marble and should be tightly attached so as not to come off.
6. Tape the other end of the thread to the straw so that the ball of foil hangs straight down from the straw, right next to the edge of the pan.
7. Tape the straw to the cup so that it doesn't move around.
8. Now that you've made the electroscope, it's time to test it with various objects.
9. To test the electroscope, create some static electricity.
10. One way to create static is by rubbing a balloon on a styrofoam plate. When you do this, you "charge" the plate.

11. Place the charged styrofoam plate on a non-metal table and place the electroscope you made on top of the styrofoam plate, being careful to only touch the electroscope by the styrofoam cup (if you touch the metal itself, you will discharge the electroscope).

12. To discharge the electroscope, touch the aluminum pie pan with your finger.

13. Charge other objects using the balloon, your hair, or wool fabric.

14. Once you charge them, place them on the styrofoam plate and place the electroscope on top, again being careful to only hold the electroscope by the styrofoam cup.

The Science Behind It

All matter is made of atoms, and all atoms are made of positively-charged protons and negatively-charged electrons. The protons are kept inside the nucleus by the strong nuclear force, while the electrons are free to move.

Static electricity results when an object accumulates a surplus of electrons, or negative charge. For example, on a dry day, you can accumulate a surplus of negative charge by rubbing your shoes in carpet. I'm sure you've experienced the feeling of getting (or giving) an electric shock. This happens when the surplus of negative charge you acquire is conducted to another object. Often this other object is made of metal, because metals are good conductors of electric charge.

In the electroscope you made, the electrons from the "charged" object will travel from the styrofoam plate through the aluminum plate, and up to the aluminum ball. Since both aluminum objects have surplus negative charge, they will repel each other.

Source:
http://nuclearconnect.org/in-the-classroom/for-teachers/making-atoms-visible-electroscope

Discovering Radioactivity

Introduction

If you want to "see" and measure the radioactivity around you, you will need a Geiger counter. Geiger counters measure ionizing radiation. They are not cheap, though some of the older 1950s style counters, though bulky, can be purchased on eBay.

Materials
- Geiger counter
- Sources of radiation (see below)

Caution

Do this experiment with a responsible adult.
Minimize the distance, time, and proximity around radioactive materials.

Procedure

Test your Geiger counter around radioactive materials.

Sources of Radioactivity

- Granite tables and counter tops (Granite contains traces of uranium)
- Uranium glass (also known as depression glass or Vaseline glass)

You can find uranium glass in green 1930s glassware, and in Vaseline uranium glass marbles on eBay (https://www.ebay.com/sch/i.html?_nkw=vaseline+marbles).

- Fiestaware (dishes that were made with a uranium oxide glaze 1930s - 1960s).

These can be purchased on eBay or at a thrift shop (bring your Geiger counter to make sure!). Use these to test for radioactivity. Do NOT eat off them. More information about fiestaware can be found here: https://www.orau.org/ptp/collection/consumer%20products/fiesta.htm

- Luminous watch dials

Vintage watches and aircraft dials may contain radium, which was used to make them glow in the dark. Radium is far more radioactive than uranium, and emits alpha, beta, and gamma radiation. Radium watch dials can be found in antique shops. Bring a Geiger counter to make sure. Also, the radium will stop glowing in the dark long before the radium will disappear. Radium has a half-life of 1600 years. If you want to learn more about the radium that went into these watches and the women who risked their lives painting them, read "The Radium Girls" by Kate Moore.

- Uranium ore (also known as uraninite and pitchblende)

This can be purchased on eBay https://www.ebay.com/sch/i.html?_nkw=uranium+ore

and United Nuclear

https://unitednuclear.com/index.php?main_page=index &cPath=2_4

- Lantern mantles (lantern mantles before 1970 were often made with radioactive thorium)

The Science Behind It

A Geiger counter is an instrument that can detect and measure radioactivity using a Geiger Mueller (GM) tube. Radioactivity, as it passes through the GM tube, ionizes the gas within the tube. This creates a momentary burst of electrons which creates a conductive path between the wire at the center of the tube, the anode, with the wall of the tube, the cathode, resulting in its characteristic clicking sound.

Geiger counters are much better at detecting beta and gamma decay than they are at detecting alpha decay. This is because alpha particles are often too big to penetrate the Geiger-Muller tube.

Source: https://mightyohm.com/blog/2012/02/feed-your-geiger-readily-available-radioactive-test-sources/

Marshmallow Radioactivity

Introduction

In this activity, you will use marshmallows to simulate radioactive decay.

Materials

- Water, 1 cup
- Food coloring, 1/2 to 1 bottle (pink and yellow)
- Toothpicks, undyed
- Ziploc bags
- 14 large marshmallows (to represent the protons and neutrons)
- 1 mini-marshmallow (to represent the beta particle)
- Styrofoam tray
- Glue
- Flashlight
- Pipe cleaners
- Marker

Caution

Prepare the marshmallows ahead of time and let dry for a few days before doing the activity.

Procedure (Preparation)

1. Prepare a mixture of pink food coloring and water and a separate mixture of yellow food coloring and water.

2. Stick a toothpick in each of the large marshmallows, and dip each of 7 marshmallows into the pink food coloring and each of the other 7 marshmallows into the yellow food coloring.

3. Stick the dyed marshmallows into a styrofoam tray to dry.

4. Let dry for several days or until not sticky to the touch.

5. Also let the mini-marshmallow air dry as well.

6. The pink marshmallows will represent the protons. Once dry, draw a "+" on each of the protons.

7. The yellow marshmallows will represent the neutrons.

8. Remove the toothpicks from each marshmallow.

9. Draw a negative "-" sign on the mini-marshmallow. This will be the beta particle.

10. Place the 14 colored marshmallows and the mini-marshmallow into a Ziploc bag.

Procedure (Activity)

1. Select 2 protons (pink marshmallows) and 2 neutrons (yellow marshmallows). Use toothpicks and glue to join these into a group of four. This represents an alpha particle.

2. Stick a toothpick into the negative particle and glue the other end of the toothpick into another pink proton

(not one that's part of the alpha particle). A positive particle plus a negative particle makes a neutron.

3. Put the alpha particle from step #1 into an empty Ziploc bag. Add 4 protons (pink) and 4 unmarked neutrons (yellow). Close the bag. This bag represents the nucleus of a stable atom.

4. What is the atomic number, mass number, name, and element symbol of this stable atom?

5. Open the bag. Add one neutron (yellow) and the neutron that was made in step #2. This is now an unstable atom because it has too many neutrons. Do NOT close this bag.

6. What is the atomic number, mass number, name, and element symbol of this unstable atom?

7. To become stable, the nucleus will emit a beta particle. Find the neutron you made in step #2. Pull off the mini-marshmallow (now it is a beta particle) and toss it about 1-2 feet from you. Leave the remaining proton in the bag and zip it closed. The atom's nucleus has changed and is stable again.

8. What is the atomic number, mass number, name, and element symbol of this newly stable atom?

9. In another Ziploc bag, place the alpha particle, along with 2 additional protons, and 2 additional neutrons.

11. What is the atomic number, mass number, name, and element symbol of this atom?

12. Now, simulate the emission of an alpha particle by removing and throwing the alpha particle from the bag.

13. What is the atomic number, mass number, name, and element symbol of this newly stable atom?

The Science Behind It

Each Ziploc bag represents an atom's nucleus.

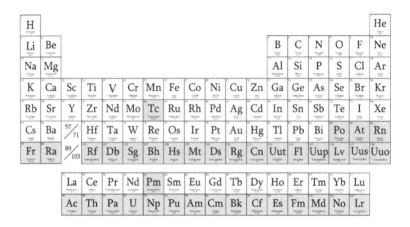

Step #4. The atom represented by 6 protons and 6 neutrons is carbon-12.

$$^{12}_{6}C$$

Because it has 6 protons, its atomic number is 6. Because it has 6 neutrons, its mass number is 12.

Recall that the mass number is the sum of the number of protons and number of neutrons.

Step #6. When two neutrons are added to carbon-12, it becomes carbon-14.

Since no additional protons are added, its atomic number doesn't change. But, with the addition of 2 neutrons, its mass number increases by 2.

Step #8. Carbon-14 decays by beta decay. When a beta particle is emitted from carbon-14, it changes one of its neutrons into a proton. Since its number of protons increases by 1, it becomes nitrogen-14. Its mass number doesn't change because the total number of protons plus neutrons doesn't change. Nitrogen-14 is a stable isotope, so it doesn't undergo radioactive decay.

$$^{14}_{6}C \rightarrow {}^{14}_{7}N + {}^{0}_{-1}e$$

Step #11. The atom represented by 4 protons and 4 neutrons is beryllium-8.

$$^{8}_{4}Be$$

Because it has 4 protons, its atomic number is 4. Because it has 4 neutrons, its mass number is 8.

Step #13. Beryllium-8 undergoes alpha decay to become helium-4.

$$^{8}_{4}\text{Be} \longrightarrow {}^{4}_{2}\text{He} + {}^{4}_{2}\text{He}$$

Actually, an alpha particle is identical to a helium nucleus. Therefore, when beryllium-8 undergoes alpha decay, it splits into 2 alpha particles (or 2 helium particles, depending on how you look at it).

Source:

http://nuclearconnect.org/in-the-classroom/for-teachers/modeling-radioactive-stable-atoms

How Much Radiation are You Exposed to in a Year?

Introduction

In this online activity, you will determine how much radiation you are exposed to in the course of a year.

Website

https://www.epa.gov/radiation/calculate-your-radiation-dose

Procedure

1. Follow the instructions on the above website to calculate your annual radiation dose.

2. You may also try this site: https://www.nrc.gov/about-nrc/radiation/around-us/calculator.html

3. These two sites are U.S.-centric. If you live outside of the United States, Google "annual radiation dose [country name]."

The Science Behind It

How much radiation is too much?

According to the above site, the average person absorbs approximately 620 mrem. What is your annual dosage?

Source:

https://www.epa.gov/radiation/calculate-your-radiation-dose

Role of Nuclear Radiation in Medicine WebQuest

Go to: https://science.howstuffworks.com/nuclear-medicine.htm#pt2

Answer the following questions:
Radiation in Medicine is used both for taking images of our insides, and for treatment of various diseases, such as cancer.

Nuclear Imaging
1. What are the 4 main nuclear medicine imagine techniques?
2. What can nuclear medicine detect?
3. Describe how Positron Emission Tomography (PET) works.
4. What is a positron?
5. Why must PET scans be administered in places that are geographically close to particle accelerators?

If you would like to learn more about particle accelerators, which this TED-Ed video on YouTube: https://youtu.be/G6mmIzRz_f8

6. Compare and contrast SPECT to PET scans.
7. Describe how cardiovascular imaging works.
8. Describe how bone scanning works.

Nuclear Treatment

Radiation treatment for cancer takes advantage of the fact that cancer cells multiply much faster than normal cells. Because cancer cells multiply more rapidly, radiation targets two mechanisms cells have for responding to damaged DNA.

9. What are these two mechanisms?
10. Why is it that people undergoing radiation treatment often lose their hair and feel nauseous?

Read this article (You may need an adult's help):
https://www.health.harvard.edu/newsletter_article/R adiation-in-medicine-a-double-edged-sword

11. What is your opinion about using nuclear radiation in medicine? Are you for it, against it, and why?

Role of Nuclear Radiation in Agriculture WebQuest

Go to: https://www.epa.gov/radtown/food-irradiation

Answer the following questions:

1. Why is ionizing radiation used in our food?
2. List 3 ways food irradiation keeps our food safe.
3. List 3 dangers that food irradiation cannot protect us from.
4. How does food irradiation work?
5. Does irradiating food make it radioactive?

This website says that NASA astronauts eat food that has been irradiated to avoid any chance of foodborne illness in space. If you want to learn more about astronauts' diet, go to:

https://spaceflight.nasa.gov/shuttle/reference/factsheets/food.html

Go to: https://www.fda.gov/food/buy-store-serve-safe-food/food-irradiation-what-you-need-know

After reading the article answer the following questions:

6. Describe the 3 ways food can be irradiated.
7. Describe or draw the symbol that indicates a food has been irradiated.

Go to:

https://www.scientificamerican.com/article/food-irradiation-salmonella-ecoli/

After reading the article answer the following questions:

8. Why don't we irradiate more food?
9. In your opinion, is food irradiation safe?

Critical Mass (Ping Pong Balls)

Introduction

In this activity, you will demonstrate how critical mass plays a role in determining whether a nuclear fission reaction will be controlled or uncontrolled. A controlled fission reaction occurs in a nuclear power plant. An uncontrolled fission reaction occurs in an atomic bomb, or nuclear meltdown.

For this activity, the larger the number of participants, the better the results. If you don't have at least four people, you may want to substitute the Critical Mass Domino activity instead.

Materials

- 2 ping pong balls per participant

Caution:

Only throw ping pong balls up in the air. Never throw them at someone else.

Procedure

1. Each participant holds a ball in each hand.
2. One person begins by throwing both balls up in the air without aiming at others.

3. When you are hit by a ball, throw your balls straight up into the air.

4. Do NOT throw your balls up in the air unless you are hit by a ball.

5. Continue until there are no more balls up in the air.

6. Run various trials in which you vary the number of participants (which represents changing the number of uranium-235 atoms), and vary the distance between the participants.

7. Time and record how long each reaction lasts, ending when the last ball is thrown in the air.

Answer the following question:

Atomic bombs are designed to trigger an uncontrollable chain reaction. Nuclear power plants are designed to control their nuclear reactions. Based on what you learned in this ping pong ball activity, how could a nuclear power plant prevent an uncontrolled chain reaction?

The Science Behind It

Nuclear fission describes the splitting of an atom's nucleus into two roughly equal halves. The first atomic bomb was made from uranium-235, which is the uranium isotope that undergoes fission. To induce fission, its nucleus captures a slow neutron. This extra neutron causes the nucleus to become unstable. This unstable nucleus quickly splits apart into the smaller nuclei barium-141 and krypton-92, and two additional neutrons, and a large amount of energy (~200MeV per fission).

$$^{235}_{92}U \rightarrow ^{141}_{56}Ba + ^{92}_{36}He + 2 \, ^{1}_{0}n$$

The neutrons that are produced from this fission reaction can be captured by other uranium-235 atoms, which themselves undergo fission, initiating a chain reaction, much like how one domino can set off a neighboring domino in the domino effect.

A critical mass is the smallest number of uranium-235 atoms needed to sustain a nuclear chain reaction. This is determined by both the number of uranium-235 atoms present, and the spacing between them.

Atomic bombs are designed to trigger this chain reaction.

Nuclear power plants are designed to control the nuclear reactions.

Source:
https://www.ans.org/nuclear/classroom/activities/

Critical Mass (Dominos)

Introduction

In this activity, like the one before it, you will demonstrate how critical mass plays a role in determining whether a nuclear fission reaction will be controlled or uncontrolled. A controlled fission reaction occurs in a nuclear power plant. An uncontrolled fission reaction occurs in an atomic bomb, or nuclear meltdown.

You do not need more than one participant for this activity.

Materials
- Set of dominos
- Ruler

Procedure

1. Arrange two straight lines of dominos so that when the first domino topples, the next one topples, and so on.

2. Topple the first line.

3. While placing a ruler between any two dominos, topple the second line and watch what happens.

4. Arrange a third line so that the dominos are spaced far enough to barely (if at all) topple the next one, and watch what happens when you topple the line.

Answer the following question:

Nuclear power plants are designed to control their nuclear reactions by limiting the amount of radioactive isotope present, and using control rods to space them apart from each other. How do the dominos and the ruler demonstrate this?

The Science Behind It

Nuclear fission describes the splitting of an atom's nucleus into roughly equal halves. The first atomic bomb was made from enriched uranium-235, which is the uranium isotope that undergoes fission. The way it does this is by capturing a slow neutron in its nucleus, forming an unstable nucleus with an extra neutron. This unstable nucleus quickly splits apart into to smaller nuclei, such as barium-141 and krypton-92, and two or three neutrons additional neutrons, and a large amount of energy (~200MeV per fission).

$$^{235}_{92}U \rightarrow\, ^{141}_{56}Ba +\, ^{92}_{36}He + 2\,^{1}_{0}n$$

The neutrons that are produced from this fission reaction can be captured by other uranium-235 atoms, which themselves undergo fission, initiating a chain reaction, much like how one domino can set off a neighboring domino in the domino effect.

A critical mass is the smallest number of uranium-235 atoms needed to sustain a nuclear chain reaction. This is determined by both the number of uranium-235 atoms present, and the spacing between them.

Source:
http://nuclearconnect.org/in-the-classroom/for-teachers/nuclear-chain-reaction-using-dominoes

Irradiated Salt

Introduction
Irradiated salt is salt that has been irradiated with at least 180,000 RADs of gamma radiation.

Materials
- irradiated table salt (NaCl) that has been irradiated with at least 180,000 RADs of gamma radiation. (Keep in DARK container or protected from light until ready to perform demonstration.)
- frying pan or other flat-surfaced item on a hot plate
- dark room (the darker the better)
- (optional) Geiger counter

Caution
Do this experiment with a responsible adult.

You will need an adult to purchase the irradiated salt (it may be difficult to purchase if you do not represent a school or business).

Do NOT eat this salt. Although it does not emit ionizing radiation, the dose of radiation given to the salt is higher than FDA permits for this type of food, and the laboratory where it was irradiated does not meet USDA/FDA standards for food handling.

Procedure

1.   Heat a dry frying pan over a stove or hot plate.

2.   Darken the room as much as possible — the darker the better.

3.   Pour some irradiated salt into the frying pan and watch what happens. You must be fairly close as the flashes are not very bright.

4.   If you have a Geiger counter, test the irradiated salt for radiation, before and after heating.

The Science Behind It

Many food products are irradiated to remove harmful bacteria. (See Role of radiation in agriculture WebQuest). In this experiment, the salt was irradiated with gamma radiation. The electrons in the salt absorbed the gamma radiation and moved to higher energy levels, known as excited states. As a result, the salt has a brownish color. When heated, the increased motion of the salt particles allows the electrons to return to their lower energy levels, giving off the stored energy in the form of photons of visible light. Once the electrons return to their normal lower energy levels, the salt will return to its white coloring.

Food that has been irradiated is not itself radioactive. Readings from a Geiger counter should not register anything above background radiation.

Source:
https://www.ans.org/nuclear/classroom/activities/

Counting Particles

Introduction

Use an atom's atomic number and mass number to determine the number of protons, neutrons, and electrons.

Materials

- Download the worksheet Counting-Particles here: https://rocketgirls.com/worksheets

The Science Behind It

The atomic number, the whole number at the top of an element's square in the periodic table, tells you the number of protons in its nucleus. Atoms are electrically neutral, which means that they contain the same number of positively-charged protons as negatively-charged electrons. Therefore, the atomic number also tells you the number of electrons outside an atom's nucleus.

The mass number tells you the number of protons plus the number of neutrons in an atom's nucleus. To determine the number of neutrons, subtract the atomic number from the mass number. For example, let's consider sodium. Sodium has an atomic number of 11. Here is its nuclide symbol.

$$^{23}_{11}\text{Na}$$

Its atomic number tells us that it contains 11 protons in its nucleus. Because atoms are electrically neutral, an atom of sodium contains an equal number of electrons. Therefore, sodium contains 11 electrons too. To determine the number of neutrons sodium has, subtract its atomic number 11 from its mass number 23.

23 - 11 = 12 neutrons

This isotope of sodium has 12 neutrons.

Counting Particles with Ions

Introduction

Use an atom's atomic number, mass number, and charge to determine the number of protons, neutrons, and electrons.

Materials

- Download the worksheet counting-particles-ions here: https://rocketgirls.com/worksheets

The Science Behind It

Atoms are electrically neutral. If an atom has a charge, it's called an ion. The charge of the ion is written in the upper right hand corner of its symbol.

A charge of -1 means that the atom is an ion, and that it contains one more electron than proton. We already know that hydrogen has 1 proton and 1 electron. So, H⁻ must have one additional electron, or 2 electrons.

$$ {}_{1}^{1}\text{H}^{0} \quad {}_{1}^{1}\text{H}^{+} \quad {}_{1}^{1}\text{H}^{-} $$

Each of the above is a version of H-1 that has a different number of electrons.

Neutral hydrogen (no charge) has the same number of electrons as protons, 1.

H^{+1} has a +1 charge. This means it has 1 more positive charge than negative charge. This is caused by losing an electron. H^+ therefore has zero electrons.

H^{-1} has a -1 charge. This means it has 1 more negative charge than positive charge. This is caused by gaining an electron. H^- therefore has 2 electrons.

Build an Atom Online

Introduction
In this activity, you will build chemical elements from their basic building blocks.

Materials
- computer with internet

Go to the website:
https://orise.orau.gov/resources/k12/documents/harnessed-atom/build-an-atom/index.html

Procedure
1. Go to the website: https://orise.orau.gov/resources/k12/documents/harnessed-atom/build-an-atom/index.html
2. Press "Start."
3. Follow the instructions on the screen.
4. You will be directed to build a helium atom and a carbon atom.

The Science Behind It
The atomic number, the whole number at the top of an element's square in the periodic table, tells you the number of protons in its nucleus. Atoms are electrically

neutral, which means that they contain the same number of positively-charged protons as negatively-charged electrons. Therefore, the atomic number also tells you the number of electrons outside an atom's nucleus.

The mass number tells you the number of protons plus the number of neutrons in an atom's nucleus. To determine the number of neutrons, subtract the atomic number from the mass number. For example, let's consider sodium. Sodium has an atomic number of 11.

$$^{23}_{11}\text{Na}$$

Its atomic number tells us that it contains 11 protons in its nucleus. Because atoms are electrically neutral, an atom of sodium contains an equal number of electrons. Therefore, sodium contains 11 electrons too. To determine the number of neutrons sodium has, subtract its atomic number 11 from its mass number 23.

$$23 - 11 = 12 \text{ neutrons}$$

This isotope of sodium has 12 neutrons.

Source:

https://orise.orau.gov/resources/k12/documents/harnes sed-atom/build-an-atom/index.html

Build an Atom Online (PhET)

Introduction

In this activity, you will build chemical elements from their basic building blocks.

Materials

- computer with internet

Go to the website:

https://phet.colorado.edu/en/simulation/build-an-atom

Procedure

1. Go to the website:
    https://phet.colorado.edu/en/simulation/build-an-atom
3. Press the play button.
2. Select "Symbol" in the middle.
3. Add protons by dragging them into the nucleus of the atom.

    Notice how the Symbol on the right-hand side changes with the addition of each new proton. You should see that the identity of the atom changes, as does its mass number (the number on the symbol's upper left corner), its atomic number (the number on the symbol's upper left corner), and its charge (the number on the symbol's upper right corner).

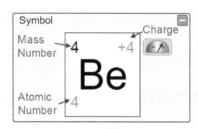

This symbol is called a nuclide symbol.

4. With each proton, the charge of the atom increases by +1. This is because your atom has no electrons. Recall that atoms are electrically neutral, so they need the same number of electrons as protons.
5. Drag enough electrons to the outside of the atom so that it is neutral.
6. Which atom did you build?
7. Add some neutrons to the atom's nucleus and notice how the mass number changes.
8. Check the box at the bottom right to show Stable/Unstable.

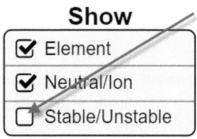

Notice how the atom becomes unstable with too many neutrons. Recall that unstable atoms are radioactive. Unstable atoms become stable by giving off particles from their nucleus.

9. Go back to the main screen and click on the "Game" and choose one or more of the games to play.

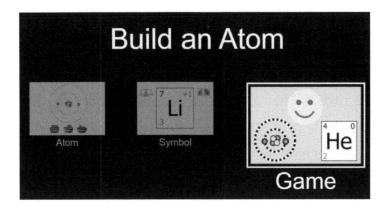

The Science Behind It

The nuclide symbol is a way of writing an element that provides its atomic number, mass number, and charge (if it has one).

$$^{23}_{11}\text{Na}$$

For this nuclide symbol, notice how sodium has an atomic number of 11, a mass number of 23 and a charge of +1.

An atomic number of 11 means that sodium has 11 protons.

A mass number of 23 means that it has a total of 23 protons and neutrons. To determine the number of neutrons, subtract the atomic number from the mass number.

23 - 11 = 12 neutrons

Atoms are electrically neutral. Since the symbol above has a charge of +1, it is called an ion. An ion is an atom with an electrical charge. A charge of +1 means that it has one more proton than electron. We already know that sodium has 11 protons. So, it must have one fewer electron, or 10 electrons.

Source:
https://phet.colorado.edu/en/simulation/build-an-atom

Make an Atomic Model (with Ping Pong Balls)

Introduction

In this activity you'll make a physical model of an atom.

Materials

- 3 colors of ping pong (or styrofoam) balls.

To determine how many balls you'll need, first choose an atom from the periodic table. The atomic number of that atom tells you how many protons you'll need (that's one color). You will need the same number of electrons (a second color). To determine the number of neutrons you'll need, round the atomic mass to the nearest whole number, and subtract from that whole number the atomic number.

For example, consider Lithium. Lithium has an atomic number of 3, so you will need 3 protons and 3 electrons. Its atomic mass is 6.94. When you round 6.94 to the nearest whole number, you get 7. 7-3 = 4 neutrons.

THE CASE OF THE MISSING URANIUM

- String
- Cardboard large enough to accommodate the model
- Glue

Procedure

1. Choose an atom from the periodic table. Note that the higher the atomic number, the more protons, neutrons, and electrons (i.e., ping pong balls) you'll need.
2. Glue together the balls that represent the protons and neutrons. You want to arrange them in an alternating pattern. This is the nucleus.
3. Glue the nucleus to the center of the cardboard.
4. Determine how many rings you need for the electrons. The ring closest to the nucleus can hold 2 electrons. The ring after that can hold 8 electrons. The ring after that (the third ring) can hold 18 electrons. And the ring after that (the fourth ring) can hold 32 electrons.
5. Glue the string around the nucleus to make however many energy level rings you need to fit all your atom's electrons.
6. Glue the electrons to the rings, evenly spaced. Make sure to fill the electrons according to Step 4.

The Science Behind It

The atom consists of three subatomic particles, the protons, neutrons, and electrons. The protons and neutrons are contained within the nucleus, whereas the electrons orbit outside the nucleus.

The number of protons is equal to the atomic number. Since atoms are neutral, meaning they have no net charge, the number of negatively-charged electrons equals the number of positively-charged protons.

For the purposes of this lab, to determine the number of neutrons your atom has, round the atomic mass to the nearest whole number. Subtract the atomic number from this rounded number to get the number of neutrons.

This is a shortcut for determining the number of neutrons an atom on the periodic table has. Unfortunately, it leads to misconceptions. The atomic mass on the periodic table represents the average atomic mass of all the naturally occurring isotopes of that element, weighted by their average. Isotopes are atoms with the same number of protons but differing numbers of neutrons. Your grade point average (GPA) is also a weighted average. If you earned 3 As and 1 B, your GPA would be higher than if you earned 2 As and 2 Bs. This is why the atomic mass on the periodic table is not a whole number. Most elements on the periodic have more than one naturally occurring isotope.

For example, there are three naturally occurring isotopes of carbon.

$$^{12}_{6}C \quad ^{13}_{6}C \quad ^{14}_{6}C$$

Each atom of carbon has 6 protons. If it had more than 6 or fewer than 6 protons, it wouldn't be carbon. The difference among these three isotopes is the number of neutrons. To determine the number of neutrons, subtract the atomic number from the mass number:

	Carbon-12	Carbon-13	Carbon 14
Mass Number	12	13	14
(Minus) Atomic Number	-6	-6	-6
Number of Neutrons	= 6 neutrons	= 7 neutrons	= 8 neutrons

When you look at carbon on the periodic table, you'll see that its average atomic mass is around 12.01, which is very close to the mass number 12.

Since the atomic mass 12.01 is the average of all the naturally occurring isotopes of carbon, weighted by their average, you can tell that the most abundant isotope is Carbon-12. Just as, if your GPA were 3.94, you could tell that you have far more As than Bs.

Sources:
https://education.jlab.org/qa/atom_model.html
https://science.howstuffworks.com/innovation/scientific-experiments/how-to-make-model-of-atom.htm

Make a Paper Plate Atomic Model

Introduction

In this activity, you will build a model of an atom using paper plates and various craft supplies you probably have lying around the house.

Materials
- Paper plate, 1, preferably chinet
- 3 different colors of pom poms, enough to represent the number of protons, electrons, and neutrons in the atom you choose.
- glue
- marker

Procedure
1. Choose an atom from the Periodic Table to model. (It's easiest to choose an atom from the among the first two rows of atoms).
2. Designate one color of pom poms for the protons, another color for the neutrons, and a third color for the electrons.
3. Determine the number of protons, neutrons, and electrons in your atom. Recall that the number

of protons and number of electrons is equal to the atomic number. The number of neutrons is equal to the atom's mass number minus its atomic number. You can search online for the mass number of a particular isotope, or you can round the atomic mass instead to find the mass number of the most abundant isotope. This rounded atomic mass minus the atomic number will give you the number of neutrons.

4. Use the glue to paste the protons and neutrons to the center of the paper plate.

5. Use a marker to draw a ring around the nucleus (the groove in a chinet plate works perfectly for this). This represents the first energy level or ring within which the electrons orbit the nucleus. This first ring can hold at most 2 electrons. Glue your first two electrons to this first ring, evenly spaced across from each other. NOTE: If you choose hydrogen as your atom, it only has 1 electron, so you should only glue one electron on this ring.

6. If your atom contains more than two electrons, draw another ring around the nucleus on the outer edge of the plate.

7. Paste the remaining electrons (up to 8) around this outer ring.

8. If you choose to make an atom that has more than 10 electrons total, you will need to draw

additional rings. The ring closest to the nucleus can hold 2 electrons. The ring after that can hold 8 electrons. The ring after that (the third ring) can hold 18 electrons. And the ring after that (the fourth ring) can hold 32 electrons.

The Science Behind It

See "Make an Atomic Model with Ping Pong Balls"

Source:

https://www.playdoughtoplato.com/atom-molecule/

Glow in the Dark Drinks

Introduction

Many people believe that radioactivity "glows in the dark." Marie Curie, who, along with her husband Pierre, discovered radium, would keep a vial of pure radium salts by her bedside to enjoy its "fairy-like glow." Though some radioactive atoms like radium do glow in the dark, not all do. And, the fact that something glows in the dark does NOT mean it's radioactive. Still, it's fun to create these "radioactive" drinks. Don't worry. They're not actually radioactive.

Materials
- UV Black Light
- Any of these drinks
- Tonic Water (produces the best glow)
- Mountain Dew™ and Diet Mountain Dew™
- Many sports drinks (such as Monster™ energy drinks, especially those that contain B vitamins)
- Some bright food coloring
- Vitamin B12 (glows bright yellow)
- Chlorophyll (from green vegetables, glows bright red)
- Milk (yellow)
- Caramel (pale yellow)

- Vanilla ice cream (pale yellow)
- Honey (golden yellow)

Procedure
1. Prepare one or more of the above drinks.
2. Turn off the lights, the darker the better.
3. Turn on the UV Black Light and watch your drink glow.

The Science Behind It

Certain substances glow under black light because of photoluminescence. Photoluminescence describes the process when electrons orbiting an atom's nucleus get excited by absorbing light energy and move to higher energy levels. When these electrons relax back to their "ground" state, they release this absorbed energy as photons of light. The two types of photoluminescence are fluorescence and phosphorescence.

Fluorescence

Fluorescence occurs when light energy, usually ultraviolet, is absorbed by an atom's electrons. This light energy is released as photons when the electrons relax back to their "ground" state. Fluorescence requires an input of light energy to "glow in the dark." And, as soon as the light source is removed, like turning off the black light, the fluorescence stops.

Phosphorescence

Phosphorescence is similar to fluorescence. The difference between the two is that, in phosphorescence, the absorbed light energy excites the electrons to even higher energy states and electrons stay in those higher energy states longer. This allows things to "glow in the dark" even after the light source is removed.

Chemiluminescence

Chemiluminescence is the process in which electrons absorb and release energy provided by a chemical reaction. In the case of glow sticks, the chemical reaction between diphenyl oxalate and hydrogen peroxide creates an unstable molecule that decomposes into carbon dioxide and energy. The energy from the decomposition excites the electrons in the included dye molecules, which release light as they relax back to their "ground" state.

Source:
https://www.thoughtco.com/glow-in-the-dark-drinks-3976053

Glow in the Dark Mountain Dew™

Introduction

Many people believe that radioactivity "glows in the dark." Marie Curie, who, along with her husband Pierre, discovered radium, would keep a vial of pure radium salts by her bedside to enjoy its "fairy-like glow." Though some radioactive atoms like radium do glow in the dark, not all do. And, the fact that something glows in the dark does NOT mean that it's radioactive. In this activity, you will make a glow-in-the-dark bottle of mountain dew, without the help of a UV black light.

Materials

- glowstick
- scissors
- 20-ounce bottle of Mountain Dew™ and Diet Mountain Dew™
- hydrogen peroxide
- dishwashing liquid
- baking soda

Caution

An adult should help with cutting open the glowstick and pouring its contents into the Mountain Dew™ bottle, and in handling the hydrogen peroxide.

Avoid getting the contents of the glowstick, or the hydrogen peroxide, in your eye.

If you get any of the glowstick's contents on your skin, wash with soap and water immediately.

Procedure

1. Empty all but 1/4-inch of the Mountain Dew™ from its bottle.
2. Squirt some dishwashing liquid into the remaining soda in the bottle.
3. Activate the glowstick.
4. Cut open one end of the glowstick and empty it into the Mountain Dew™ bottle.
5. Add 1 to 3 capfuls of hydrogen peroxide.
6. Add a pinch of baking soda and seal the bottle immediately.
7. Shake the bottle vigorously, turn off the lights, and watch it glow.

The Science Behind It

This reaction is an example of chemiluminescence. Chemiluminescence is the process in which electrons absorb and release energy provided by a chemical reaction. In the case of glow sticks, the chemical reaction between diphenyl oxalate and hydrogen peroxide creates an unstable molecule that decomposes into carbon dioxide and energy. The energy from the decomposition excites the electrons in the included dye molecules, which release light as they relax back to their "ground" state. The chemiluminescence is further aided by the energy released from the reaction between baking soda and hydrogen peroxide.

Source:
https://www.thoughtco.com/glow-in-the-dark-mountain-dew-607628

What Makes an Atom Unstable?

Introduction

Why are some atoms stable, whereas others are radioactive? In this activity, you will watch a video explaining the difference between stable and unstable nuclei and answer some fill-in-the-blank questions.

Materials

- Video: https://youtu.be/UtZw9jfIxXM
- Worksheet stable-and-unstable: https://rocketgirls.com/worksheets

Procedure

Watch the video and complete the worksheet.

Source:
https://youtu.be/UtZw9jfIxXM

Irradiated Radishes: The Effects of Irradiation on Seed Germination

Introduction

Some agriculture is irradiated to kill off harmful bacteria. Agriculture that is exposed to radiation in this way is not itself radioactive. In this activity, you will observe the effect of different levels of irradiation on radish seeds.

Materials

- Irradiated radish seeds. These can be ordered online at Carolina.com (https://www.carolina.com/plant-genetics/radish-irradiated-seed-set-5-pks-of-50/179146.pr?question=irradiated+seeds) or Amazon.
- Clear CD "jewel" cases, 5 - 15
- Paper towels
- Permanent marker
- Scotch tape
- Modeling clay, enough to hold the CD cases upright
- Tray in which to hold the CD cases
- Eyedropper
- Graph paper

Caution
Do NOT eat the seeds, or the growing radish rootlets.

Procedure
The irradiated radish seeds come in 4 sets - 50 Krads, 150 Krads 500, and 4,000 Krads. (NOTE: Krads stands for kilorads, which is equal to 1000 rads).

1. Label the CD cases as follows:
   a. Case 1: Control (no irradiation)
   b. Case 2: 50 Krads
   c. Case 3: 150 Krads
   d. Case 4: 500 Krads
   e. Case 5: 4,000 Krads
2. Fold a paper towel to fit into each one of these CD cases.
3. Using the eyedropper, dampen each paper towel so that it is fully covered in water but not dripping.
4. Place the paper towels into the jewel cases.
5. Place six seeds of the labeled dose, on the paper towel in each CD case, toward the top to allow room for the roots to grow downward.
6. The seeds should be between the plastic cover of the jewel case and the paper towel.
7. Place them along the top so that the rootlets have room to grow. The CD cases will be placed

vertically upright, so the roots can grow downward.

8. Close up each CD class with a small piece of Scotch tape.

9. Use the modeling clay to stand each case upright in the tray, remembering that the seeds themselves should be toward the top. The CDs should be spaced enough apart from each other that you can view them without removing them from the tray.

10. Add a small piece of Scotch tape around each edge to make sure the CDs stay closed.

11. Place the CDs upright on the tray. Use the modeling clay to hold them in a vertical position. Separate them so that they are several inches apart, and you can easily view the seeds.

12. Keep the jewel cases at a temperature between 16°C and 22°C (60–70°F) and out of direct sunlight. You want to keep the same conditions for all seeds.

13. Record the date and time that you started the experiment.

14. Observe the seeds over the course of the next week.

15. Keep the paper towels damp, using the eye dropper to carefully add water to the paper towels, as often as necessary. Reseal the cases with tape each time, to keep the cases closed.

16. Try to keep the conditions (light, temperature, amount of water added) the same for all the seeds. Record all procedures and data in your lab notebook.

17. Over the course of the week, record how many seeds germinate (sprout), and record your observations about the appearance of the growing rootlets, at least twice a day.

18. Make sketches or take pictures of the seeds twice per day.

19. Record the length of the rootlets.

20. The last day of the week, graph the germination rate (in percent) vs. the irradiation dose. The irradiation dose is the independent variable, so it should be plotted on the x-axis. The germination rate is the dependent variable, so it should be plotted on the y-axis.

21. For example, if 4 out of 6 seeds germinate, the germination rate is 67 percent.

22. Also, graph the average length of the rootlets vs. irradiation dose. Again, the irradiation dose is the independent variable, so it belongs on the x-axis.

Questions to Answer

1. Looking at your graphs, did the irradiation dose affect the germination rate?

2. Why do you think this is?

3. Did the irradiation dose affect the rootlet length?

4. Why do you think this is?

Extension

1. Do this experiment two more times, with fresh materials, to get a set of three trials. You may run all three trials simultaneously. Average your results.

The Science Behind It

Radiation is used in agriculture to destroy harmful bacteria. These radish seeds were exposed to varying levels of gamma radiation. Gamma radiation is a form of ionizing radiation. Ionizing radiation is radiation that produces ions by removing electrons from atoms and molecules. Some of these ions that are formed become free radicals which are known to be damaging to tissues, and especially destructive to DNA, causing mutations and other structural damage.

In agriculture, they usually only irradiate the harvest, not the seeds. Since the DNA of these seeds was damaged due to radiation, it should affect the plants that sprout from them.

Source:

https://www.sciencebuddies.org/science-fair-projects/project-ideas/PlantBio_p039/plant-biology/effects-of-irradiation-on-seed-germination#procedure

Find a Nuclear Reactor Near You

Introduction

You may have a nuclear power plant in your backyard without knowing it. In this activity, you'll identify how far you live from the nearest nuclear reactor, and how much radiation you experience as a result.

Materials

- For the United States, go to the website: https://www.nrc.gov/info-finder/region-state/index.html
- If you are outside the United States, Google: "nuclear reactor near me"

Procedure

1. Go to the website https://www.nrc.gov/info-finder/region-state/index.html and select the state you live in.
2. Find the "Operating Nuclear Power Reactors."
3. Click on the hyperlink for each operating nuclear power reactor and use Google maps to find out how far the reactor is from you.
4. To do this, open Google maps in another browser tab.

5. Copy and paste the name of the reactor into Google maps.
6. Press "Enter."
7. To find how far the nuclear power plant is from you, select "Directions."
8. Type in your address as your location and select "Leave now."

The Science Behind It

How far are you from a nuclear reactor? And how does that affect you?

First a little background...

Alpha particles only travel a few inches. They get stopped by paper and skin.

Beta particles can travel up to 10 feet. They get stopped by wood, thick plastic, or even a ream of paper.

Gamma rays, which aren't particles at all, can travel large distances at the speed of light. Fortunately, they lose half their energy for every 500 feet. This means that, if you live 1000 feet from a nuclear reactor, gamma particles that haven't already been stopped would only have 1/4 of their energy.

One mile is over 5000 feet. If you lived one mile from a nuclear power plant, and a gamma particle for some reason was able to reach you without being blocked, it would only have about 1/1024th of its original energy.

The thing is, nuclear power plants in the U.S. have many safety measures in place to prevent an accident like the one on Three Mile Island. Even if a reactor melted down, in which it released radiation into the air due to an uncontrollable chain reaction, only the 10 miles around it would be evacuated. This is called the plume ingestion pathway.

50 miles from the power plant is referred to as the plume exposure pathway.

If radiation is leaking from a nuclear reactor, it would show up in the vegetation within the first 10 miles, which is why the vegetation is tested regularly.

It may assure you to know that eating a banana exposes you to more radiation than living 50 miles from a nuclear power plant. See this site to learn about "banana equivalent: doses"" https://www.universityofcalifornia.edu/longform/what-know-you-go-bananas-about-radiation

Source:
https://www.nrc.gov/info-finder/region-state/index.html

Find a Nuclear Test Site Near You

Introduction

You may live very close to a nuclear test site, where atomic bombs have been detonated. The very first detonation of an atomic bomb New Mexico occurred on July 16, 1945. Since then, there have been 2055 more test explosions. In this activity, you'll identify how far you live from a nuclear test site, and how much radiation you experience as a result.

Materials
- Website:
  https://www.atomicarchive.com/almanac/test-sites/testing-map.html

Procedure
1. Go to the website:
   https://www.atomicarchive.com/almanac/test-sites/testing-map.html
2. Click on a nuclear symbol near where you live.
3. The site will tell you what tests were performed there and when.
4. There are several web-based resources to learn about the effects of the fallout (radioactive

particles released from a nuclear explosion) from these tests.

5. The Center for Disease Control (CDC) devotes a page on its website to the effects of radioactive fallout from nuclear testing here: https://www.cdc.gov/nceh/radiation/fallout/rf-gwt_home.htm

6. The National Cancer Institute provides information about the effects of I-131 exposure from nuclear testing here: https://www.cancer.gov/about-cancer/causes-prevention/risk/radiation/i-131

7. You can calculate your thyroid dose and risk from US detonations here: https://radiationcalculators.cancer.gov/fallout/

8. Here's a fascinating article about those affected by the Nevada test site, including claims that the famous actor John Wayne may be among them: https://www.atomicheritage.org/history/nevada-test-site-downwinders

The Science Behind It

According to the calculator at cancer.gov, anyone living in the United States between the years 1951 and 1982 may have been exposed to increased levels of radiation due to fallout from nuclear testing. The site goes on to say that, "if you were born after 1982, your estimated thyroid dose from nuclear weapons testing is negligibly small and the calculator would not be relevant to you." You may be too young to have been affected, but not your parents and grandparents.

In the 1940s through the 1960s, various sites in the U.S. were designated as nuclear test sites. The fallout from these tests was carried throughout the U.S. by wind and rainfall. Some areas, such as Nevada itself, Utah, Colorado, Idaho, and Montana, received the bulk of this fallout. The fallout created an excess of the unstable isotope I-131 in the grass and vegetation in these areas. The cows and goats in these regions that consumed the contaminated grass produced milk contaminated with I-131. Those most affected appear to be children who drank large quantities of fresh milk between 1951 and 1982.

The iodine from the milk gets taken up by the thyroid gland and can lead to thyroid disease and even thyroid cancer, though the latter is rare.

The thyroid is located in the front of your neck under the skin. To find it, touch your throat in your Adam's apple area with one finger, and touch your other finger to the top of your breastbone. Your thyroid is between your two fingers. It bobs up and down when you swallow.

The thyroid's role in your body is to regulate hormones, which are chemicals that direct your body to perform the right functions at the right time. The thyroid plays a large part in your metabolism, which is how fast your body can produce and use energy, and in your physical growth.

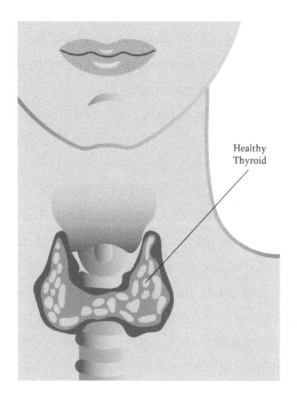

Healthy
Thyroid

The thyroid gland needs iodine to function. As your body does not itself produce iodine, the gland gets its iodine from your diet. Iodine is such an important mineral in your diet, that it was added to salt (iodized salt) in 1924, which effectively eliminated the diseases cause by iodine deficiency, such as goiter, which is an enlarged thyroid, and cretinism (look it up).

Source:
https://www.atomicarchive.com/almanac/test-sites/testing-map.html

Nuclear Fission Simulation

Introduction

In this activity, you will simulate the process of nuclear fission and its application in the atomic bomb and in nuclear reactors.

Materials

- Website: https://phet.colorado.edu/en/simulation/legacy/nuclear-fission
  NOTE: This simulation may not work on a chrome book or mobile device.

Procedure

1. Go to: https://phet.colorado.edu/en/simulation/legacy/nuclear-fission
2. Press the play button to begin the simulation.
3. The tab "Fission: One Nucleus" should be displayed.
4. Fire a neutron at the nucleus and watch what happens.
5. "Reset Nucleus" to begin again.
6. What is the nuclide symbol for the starting nucleus?

7. What is the nuclide symbol for the nucleus as soon as it absorbs a neutron?

8. What happens after the nucleus absorbs a neutron?

9. Describe the process of nuclear fission, based on what you saw in the visualization.

10. Switch tabs to "Chain Reaction."

11. Add 10 U-235 nuclei to the chamber.

12. Describe what happens once a neutron is fired into the chamber.

13. Do all the U-235 nuclei undergo fission? Why or why not?

14. Select "Reset All" at the bottom right of the simulation.

15. Add 25 U-235 nuclei to the chamber.

16. Describe what happens once a neutron is fired into the chamber.

17. Do all the U-235 nuclei undergo fission? Why or why not?

18. Select "Reset All" at the bottom right of the simulation.

19. Add 25 U-235 nuclei to the chamber.

20. Describe what happens once a neutron is fired into the chamber.

21. Do all the U-235 nuclei undergo fission? Why or why not?

22. Select "Reset All" at the bottom right of the simulation.

23. Add 100 U-235 nuclei to the chamber.

24. Describe what happens once a neutron is fired into the chamber.

25. Do all the U-235 nuclei undergo fission? Why or why not?

26. Which generated the most energy, 10 U-235 nuclei, 25 U-235 nuclei, or 100 U-235 nuclei? Explain your answer.

27. Switch tabs to "Nuclear Reactor."

28. Press "Fire Neutrons" at least 10 times in a row to simulate how a nuclear reactor generates energy through nuclear fission.

29. Compare and contrast what you observed in the "Chain Reaction" tab. What was similar? What was different? Why?

30. Select "Reset Nuclei."

31. Grab and drag the handle on the right about half-way down:

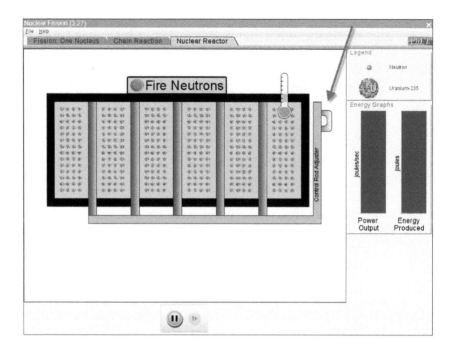

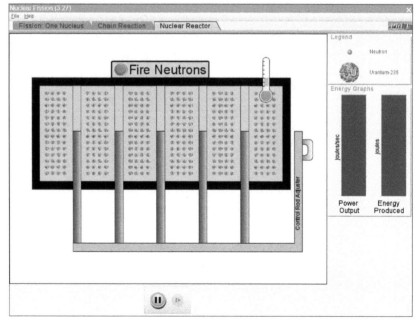

32. Press "Fire Neutrons" at least 10 times in a row.

33. Compare and contrast Step 32 to Step 28.
34. What role do you think the control rods play in a nuclear reactor?
35. Select "Reset Nuclei."
36. Now, grab and drag the handle on the right all the way down.
37. Press "Fire Neutrons" at least 10 times in a row.
38. Compare and contrast Step 37 to Steps 28 and 32.

Extension:

Nuclear reactors use control rods to prevent an uncontrollable chain reaction. If such an uncontrollable nuclear reaction takes place, it can lead to a nuclear meltdown. Research the nuclear accidents at Three Mile Island and the Fukushima Daiichi nuclear power plant in Japan.

The Science Behind It

Nuclear fission is the process in which an atom splits in roughly two halves, releasing a tremendous amount of energy.

The process of nuclear fission starts when a large nucleus absorbs a neutron, creating a very unstable intermediate nucleus with one too many neutrons. This unstable intermediate nucleus cannot hold, and eventually splits apart into two halves.

A chain reaction occurs when the U-235 nucleus, undergoing fission, releases additional neutrons, which are then absorbed by neighboring U-235 nuclei, causing them to undergo fission too.

The chain reaction is controlled when the concentration of fissionable nuclei is low, or by the insertion of control rods, which cool off and slow the particles down.

This chain reaction can be intensified by increasing the number of U-235 nuclei around, which is accomplished by enriching uranium. The atomic bomb dropped on Hiroshima was fueled by the nuclear fission of U-235.

Source:
https://phet.colorado.edu/en/simulation/legacy/nuclear -fission

Take an Atomic Heritage Tour

Introduction

The website curated by Atomic Heritage has many different "tours" you can go on to learn more about the discovery of radioactivity and the Manhattan Project. The Manhattan Project was the code name for the United States' development of the atomic bomb during World War II.

Materials

- website: https://www.atomicheritage.org/tours

Procedure

1. Go to the website: https://www.atomicheritage.org/tours
2. Go on any one or more of their "tours," including the discovery of radioactivity, the various sites in which the atomic bomb was developed, Japanese first-hand narratives, and the spies that were deployed to find out how close Nazi Germany was to developing the bomb themselves.

The Science Behind It

Physicists immediately realized the destructive capabilities of nuclear power as soon as word spread that

Otto Hahn and Lise Meitner in Germany had discovered nuclear fission in 1938. From that moment on, the race to make the atomic bomb began. Albert Einstein himself wrote a letter to President Franklin D. Roosevelt warning him about how dangerous it would be if Germany developed the bomb first. As a result, President Roosevelt immediately formed an Advisory Committee on Uranium, composed of scientists and military personnel to investigate the matter.

Since nuclear fission was discovered in Germany by German physicists, Germany had a running start in developing the bomb.

Therefore, even as the Manhattan Project was developing the bomb, many were worried that they were too late. So, they sent spies into Germany to find out how far along the Germans were.

As it turned out, the Germans were not close to developing the bomb by the time Germany surrendered, perhaps because many of Germany's best physicists had already been expelled from the country and were working on behalf of the United States.

Source:
https://www.atomicheritage.org/tours

Rocket Girls

Glossary

Glossary

Alpha Decay - the giving off of an alpha particle from the nucleus of an unstable atom.

Alpha Particle - a particle made of two protons and two neutrons that is released from the nucleus of an unstable atom.

Atomic Number - the number of protons an atom has, usually written at the top of each element in the Periodic Table.

Background Radiation - the natural radiation we're exposed to on a regular basis, consisting of cosmic radiation from the universe, the radiation from naturally occurring radioactive isotopes, as well as the radiation from x-rays, and nuclear events such as nuclear weapons and nuclear accidents.

Beta Decay - the giving off of a beta particle from the nucleus of an unstable atom.

Beta Particle - A beta particle has the same mass and charge as an electron but comes from an atom's nucleus.

Cathode Ray - a beam of electrons emitted from the cathode of a high-vacuum tube.

Chemiluminescence - a process in which energy from a chemical reaction is absorbed by exciting electrons to higher energy levels. As the electrons relax back down to their "ground state," the energy is released relatively slowly in the form of photons of light.

Critical Mass - the smallest amount of fissile material (such as uranium-235) needed to sustain a nuclear chain reaction.

Electromagnetic Radiation - a flow of energy that travels at the speed of light, which includes visible light, radio waves, x-rays, and gamma radiation. It consists of waving electric and magnetic fields.

Electron - negatively-charged particle outside the nucleus of an atom.

Excited State - when an electron absorbs enough energy, it will move to higher energy levels, or rings, further away from the nucleus.

Fallout - radioactive particles released from a nuclear explosion or accident.

Fissile - an atom that can undergo nuclear fission.

Fluorescence - a process in which energy is absorbed by a substance by exciting its electrons to higher energy levels. As the electrons relax back down to their "ground state," the energy is released quickly in the form of photons of light.

Gamma Decay - gamma radiation, a high energy form of electromagnetic radiation, given off by radioactive atoms.

Ground State - the lowest energy level an electron can occupy.

Half-Life - the time it takes for half of a radioactive sample to decay into its daughter nuclei.

Ion - an atom with an electrical charge.

Ionizing Radiation - radiation that produces ions by removing electrons from atoms and molecules.

Isotopes - two or more atoms of the same element with different mass numbers.

Matter - anything that has mass and takes up space.

Mass number - the number of protons and neutrons in the nucleus of an atom.

Neutron - particle with no charge (neutral) in the nucleus of an atom, with the same mass as a proton.

Nuclear Fission - the process in which an atom splits in roughly two halves, releasing a tremendous amount of energy.

Nucleus - the small, dense, positively-charged center of an atom.

Nuclide Symbol - an element's symbol preceded by its mass and atomic numbers.

Periodic Table - a table of all the known chemical elements organized by atomic number and repeating chemical properties.

Phosphorescence - a process in which energy is absorbed by a substance by exciting its electrons to higher energy levels. As the electrons relax back down to their "ground state," the energy is released relatively slowly in the form of photons of light.

Positron - a positively-charged beta particle from the nucleus of an unstable atom.

Positron Decay - the giving off of a positron from the nucleus of an unstable atom.

Proton - positively-charged particle in the nucleus of an atom. The number of protons in an atom's nucleus determines the identity of the atom.

Radioactivity - the giving off of particles and energy from the nucleus of an unstable atom.

Shielding – blocking radiation from reaching you.

NOW AVAILABLE

Book 2:

All That Glitters isn't Gold

The **Second Book** of the Rocket Girls Series.

Due to an unfortunate lab accident, Sam must replace
Kimberly's gold bracelet. The more she learns about gold,
however, the more she realizes there's something not quite
right. Does she risk losing her friendship with Kimberly to
uncover the truth?

ABOUT THE AUTHOR

Melanie Fine is an author, high school chemistry teacher, and cantor on a mission to share the stories of women scientists who have contributed beyond their measure without due recognition. Their stories teach us that all things are possible. She lives in Los Angeles with her son. Follow her @RocketGirlsSci

Lightning Source UK Ltd.
Milton Keynes UK
UKHW022347120821
388717UK00002B/319